# The
# product-led organization

Todd Olson

The
# product-led organization

Drive growth by putting
product at the center of your
customer experience

WILEY

Published by John Wiley & Sons, Inc., Hoboken, New Jersey.

Published simultaneously in Canada.

For general information on our other products and services or for technical support, please contact our Customer Care Department within the United States at (800) 762–2974, outside the United States at (317) 572–3993 or fax (317) 572–4002.

Wiley publishes in a variety of print and electronic formats and by print-on-demand. Some material included with standard print versions of this book may not be included in e-books or in print-on-demand. If this book refers to media such as a CD or DVD that is not included in the version you purchased, you may download this material at http://booksupport.wiley.com. For more information about Wiley products, visit www.wiley.com.

*Library of Congress Cataloging-in-Publication Data*

Names: Olson, Todd, 1975- author.
Title: The product-led organization : drive growth by putting product at
    the center of your customer experience / Todd Olson.
Description: Hoboken, New Jersey : John Wiley & Sons, Inc., [2021] |
    Includes index.
Identifiers: LCCN 2020022830 (print) | LCCN 2020022831 (ebook) | ISBN
    9781119660873 (hardback) | ISBN 9781119660910 (adobe pdf) | ISBN
    9781119660927 (epub)
Subjects: LCSH: New products. | Product design. | Consumer behavior.
Classification: LCC HF5415.153 .O47 2021 (print) | LCC HF5415.153 (ebook)
    | DDC 658.5/75—dc23
LC record available at https://lccn.loc.gov/2020022830
LC ebook record available at https://lccn.loc.gov/2020022831

Cover Design: Wiley
Cover Image: © best_vector/Shutterstock

Printed in the United States of America

SKY10020492_081920

*To my family for all your love and support.*

*To my team members at Pendo, who inspire and motivate me.*

# Contents

# Preface

I'm a builder. I've been building and shipping software since I was 14 years old. A lot has changed since then. Like many of you, I remember when shipping software on time with a predictable level of quality was difficult. Projects (often referred to as "death marches") were often late, and reports of software that didn't sell well appeared regularly in the news. The Standish Group published a now-infamous study called the "Chaos Report," which cited that nearly 84 percent of projects will either fail or go over budget.[1] As if we needed a reminder.

The Chaos Report also said that "most features are rarely or never used." OK, so it's not just that we can't build software predictably; we're not even building the right things. Clearly, the Chaos Report was aptly named.

Much has changed, however, since the days of the Chaos Report. Agile development techniques have become the dominant mode of building software. By breaking software development into smaller chunks, Agile methodologies often help us deliver working software more predictably. These techniques and others have significantly improved the success rates of software projects—even in the midst of a global pandemic.

Another challenge in software development was distribution. It's probably hard to imagine that there was a time not all that long ago when we had to ship software on a physical medium—think CDs (remember those?)—or that we had to set up a bunch of infrastructure and manage it ourselves. This was painful and expensive. It's hard enough to build something. Now we have to dedicate people to keeping it running 24×7. The advent of cloud services, like

---

[1] "CHAOS Report," Standish Group International, 2015

Amazon Web Services (AWS), the Google Cloud Platform (GCP), and Microsoft Azure have fundamentally changed the game. Developers now develop, test, and then deploy software within minutes. Software can be distributed globally with minimal effort.

So now we can build and distribute software predictably. But what about building the right things in the first place? This is where you may imagine a cue for a record scratch. We still have a long way to go here.

In the spirit of the Chaos Report, my company, Pendo (https://www.pendo.io/), published its own report citing that only 12 percent of software is ever used. Based on our research, we've calculated that some $29.5 billion was invested in features that were never used. And that's just the money invested in public cloud projects; the number would be significantly larger if it also included software built by private companies in the cloud. That almost makes the Standish Group numbers look tame by comparison. While we've made significant progress delivering against deadlines, we're still a bit of a hot mess in deciding what to build in the first place.

After a long career of building software, I eventually found myself in product management. This is where I shifted my focus from the largely met challenge of how to deliver software on time, on budget, and with the right quality, to the largely unmet challenge of building the right things for customers. As I dug in, I saw how little progress had been made.

The Agile community describes the product owner (another name for product manager) role simply as the "onsite customer." In other words, the job of product managers is to synthesize inputs from customers, internal stakeholders, and the market to create a roadmap of what to build. Product managers uniquely sit at the intersection of engineering and sales, which gives them a significant amount of influence.

In my professional experience, I've found product people to be some of the most passionate and empathetic people on planet earth. They're wired a bit differently than the average human, possessing a certain compulsion—almost an obsession—to make things and to make them better. Perhaps this is what attracts a lot of people to this role: the general sense that this is a community of people who deeply, passionately give a darn.

The fact that they deeply, passionately care is why I'll submit that virtually every feature and every product begins with the thesis that it will meaningfully improve some aspect of a customer's work or life. Few product teams ever set off on a journey to produce anything less than that. But what begins as a clear idea toward obvious and self-evident positive impact for end users becomes more complicated when it comes time to ship code.

Agile software development has helped to accelerate the delivery of working software. Faster, more frequent releases force teams to refocus on velocity and output. DevOps extended these productivity gains downstream to clear the development/operations bottleneck that gets in the way of putting this working software into production. In doing so, it has enabled more frequent releases, delivered continuously.

All of this has accelerated the pace of innovation, to be sure, which you'd think would be a great thing for customers. In some ways, it has undoubtedly made their lives better. Companies turn out features they need much faster than ever before. But it also means that customers are getting inundated with a tidal wave of features that has the potential to overwhelm them.

This is partially an artifact of the age we live in, one of perpetual distractions. As you read these words, contemplate where you left your smartphone. If you're like me, it's probably in your pocket, in your lap, or on the side table next to your bed—never out of reach, rarely out of mind. If this is the general state of our attention spans, the fundamental rewiring of our reptilian brains, why do we expect users to stay on top of the torrent of features we're pushing at them?

I mentioned earlier that my company studies (and helps improve) the state of feature adoption—and the vast majority of features are rarely or never used. Why? In many cases, new features are like the tree falling in the woods that nobody heard. They're simply missed in the flurry of competing priorities and perpetual distractions. In other cases, they're flawed in some way—in function, in scope, or in user experience. Users simply turn up their noses.

That's why the job of engaging users is every bit as important as shipping code. The product or feature launch is just the start. Now you need to ensure that users unlock the value you had in mind in the first place. This means timing and targeting engagement to ensure that you're reaching users at the appropriate moments on their journey. And it means listening and learning, using these engagements to inch ever closer to the perfect problem/solution match for customers.

## THE PRODUCT MANAGER EMERGES

Product management has recently emerged as one of the hottest roles in tech. In his famous blog post, and now part of his book, *The Hard Thing About Hard Things: Building a Business When There Are No Easy Answers* (Harper Business, 2014), entrepreneur and venture capitalist Ben Horowitz suggests that a good product manager is one who is, in effect, the CEO of the product. That sounds like a cool job. Others seem to agree. *U.S. News and World Report* recently cited product management as one of the top five hot jobs for MBAs. In fact, it's not uncommon for newly minted MBAs to forgo hedge funds and investment banks for product management roles with Silicon Valley, cloud-based software as a service (SaaS) companies. As Robert F. Smith, the founder, chair, and CEO of private equity firm Vista Equity Partners, which owns 50 software companies and has more than 65,000 employees worldwide, framed it in an interview with *PC Magazine*, software is "the most productive tool introduced in our business lives in the past 50 years." However, what we're witnessing in the world around us isn't just a seismic shift within software companies. Now that, as famed venture capitalist Marc Andreessen foresaw, software has eaten the world,[2] product management is now seen as a training ground for future entrepreneurs, CEOs, and investors in every industry imaginable.

The challenge with building "the right thing," or rather building things that reliably deliver value to customers, is that it isn't a

---

[2]Marc Andreessen, "Why Software Is Eating The World," The Wall Street Journal, August 20, 2011

one-time event. It's not as simple as choosing the perfect thing to build and then building it. The product is never done. It's evolutionary. That means product managers have to evolve too.

To deliver on that promise requires new skills, tools, and new practices and habits—in short, a new way of thinking. It's a way of thinking that makes the product not just the thing that you sell, but the most important asset in your strategic arsenal. It's a way of thinking that focuses as much on the phase after the product is shipped as on getting the product out the door in the first place. It's a way of thinking that's intensely data driven, where measurement is continuous, and these insights guide users to get more value and guide companies to make their products better. Good product managers understand this, and books like *Four Steps to the Epiphany* by Steve Blank (K&S Ranch, 2013) and *The Lean Startup* by Eric Ries (Crown Business, 2011) have popularized new strategies for deciding what to build and then iterating to create lasting value for customers. Data-informed is now a modifier for virtually every business function, product management certainly to no lesser degree. Each year, the data our company collects from surveying product managers reveals a role that's increasingly dependent on troves of customer data and market insight. We know that product managers are relying more on data than instinct.

It's also a job that's never "done"—and certainly not when features are shipped—there is no longer any cake, pizza, or plastic tchotchkes to celebrate when the initial product is first shipped. Success is achieved when customers have fully realized the value of the product, and the product has achieved a perfect match with their needs.

For many companies, business models and the go-to-market motion are becoming product led. What exactly does that mean? It means that the product is one of the first moments of truth on a buying journey, where a trial or freemium offer becomes a first impression. It means that sales and marketing organizations are reorienting to let the product and the positive social proof it generates take the lead, where aggressive sales and marketing tactics take a backseat.

This requires a more data-informed or data-inspired approach to building digital products. By relying on data, I don't mean somehow automating the un-automatable. Fear not, there is no robot army coming to take over the jobs of product managers. What I mean is using data to inform and inspire better decisions, to build better products, and to deliver better experiences. Moreover, I mean to put products to work to drive profitable growth for your business—no matter what business you're in. It's about data in support of the product people who design, build, and evolve software that customers can't live without. That's at the root of how you become product led.

# Introducing Product-led Strategy

You can't go a day without seeing a headline about the success of companies like Apple, Netflix, Peloton, and Amazon. They've each won the hearts—and wallets—of their customers. But they've got something else in common too: **they're all product-led organizations**!

Gone are the days when product managers would check off features like some technical bean counter. Today's product leaders obsess over delivering high-value experiences at every stage of the product journey. They team with marketing to imagine the product as a customer acquisition tool; they align with sales to maximize trial-to-customer conversions; they partner with customer success to create a virtuous cycle of in-app guidance and insights. In other words, product is woven into the fabric of modern companies. We call these organizations "product led."

Product-led organizations put the product experience at the very center of everything they do, so much so that each and every function has a maniacal focus on the product, considering how people use it, how people feel about it, and how to optimize it to make every touchpoint with a customer as beneficial as possible. For a product-led company, nothing matters more than delivering a product that anticipates and answers—in a simple, intuitive, and enjoyable way—the evolving needs of its users. Ultimately, the product becomes the vehicle for acquiring and retaining customers, driving growth, and influencing organizational priorities. **The product is not just one part of the customer experience; it is the experience**. Everything your company does should lead back to your product. This means that aspects of sales, marketing, education, service, and support should converge inside the product. Your product should become the nexus of the customer experience.

But the benefits of adopting a product-led strategy go beyond building products users love. Radically reorganizing your company around your product can help increase communication, bring you closer to your customers, and improve collaboration by providing product and go-to-market teams with a common view of success—and a common vehicle to get there.

This book is meant to help you along your product-led journey. In the pages that follow, you will learn how to help transform your organization, drive growth, and advance your career.

## THE RISE OF THE PRODUCT-LED COMPANY

Product-led strategy wasn't always as prevalent as it's become more recently. Here's a prime example. Prior to starting Pendo, I worked at a company that competed against Atlassian, the now massively successful enterprise software company. That's when I experienced the power of a product-led business first-hand. Atlassian touted the fact that they were growing their business without the need for a sales team. At the time Atlassian went public in 2015, they reportedly spent just 19 percent of their revenue on sales and marketing—a fraction of the spend of similar companies.[1] The secret to their success was a great product experience delivered at an affordable price. As Jay Simon, Atlassian's president, has said, "The flywheel begins with a great product that [solves] meaningful problems for customers. And then we try to remove as much friction in front of the customer's path as possible."

In the past, companies could hide product limitations behind a smokescreen of marketing campaigns. But prioritizing new customers over ensuring your product creates successful outcomes for your existing users has a way of catching up with you. Product-led companies are more durable because their customers are more loyal. Here are a few reasons why:

---

[1] Geoffrey Keating, "How Atlassian built a $20 billion company with a unique sales model," Intercom, March 21, 2019; https://www.intercom.com/blog/podcasts /scale-how-atlassian-built-a-20-billion-dollar-company-with-no-sales-team/

## 1. The Enduring Influence of Data

Back in 1994, *Businessweek* reported that companies were collecting data, "crunching it to predict how likely you are to buy a product, and using that knowledge to craft a marketing message precisely calibrated to get you to do so."[2] The piece also admitted that most companies were actually too overwhelmed with all of the data that they were collecting to put it to use effectively. We've come a long way since then. It's now commonplace for companies—both consumer-facing and B2B—to collect and analyze massive amounts of usage information to make regular updates to their product experiences. As a result, software users have grown accustomed to constant improvement. They expect more from all of their products, whether it's online banking, a food delivery app, or software they use at work. This phenomenon, called consumerization, has upended software design.

## 2. The Crowded Path to Market

In the days before the advent of SaaS and the cloud, building a product and bringing it to market took significant investment and resources. This constrained the supply of new products. No longer. Services like AWS have lowered the technological barriers to entry, while a parallel surge in venture investments has underwritten go-to-market functions. As a result, virtually every software category has become crowded. New ideas, great tech, and splashy marketing are not enough to keep competitors at bay. Instead, delivering a product journey that customers love is how today's products thrive.

## 3. Changing Buyer Behaviors

It used to be that software purchases were driven by the CIO, CTO, or IT department. Thanks to new low-cost business models like freemium, that's not true anymore. In the coming years, 47 percent

---

[2]Jonathan Berry, "Database Marketing," *BusinessWeek*, September 5, 1994

of software purchases will be made by non-IT departments.[3] Or, as Blake Bartlett of OpenView Ventures has said, "Software just shows up in the workplace unannounced."[4] That shift in who's making the decisions to buy and use software has far-reaching implications for companies. You no longer have the luxury of controlling how users find or begin using your products. Your responsibility has to shift to creating great user experiences inside the product itself, while also stoking opportunities for conversion, retention, and cross-selling. Said another way, your product needs to become the channel where you communicate with your buyers.

## 4. The Emergence of Systems of Record

Every department, with the exception of product, has long had its own "system of record"—a cornerstone solution that helps the team perform its function and track its impact. Sales teams have customer acquisition goals and CRM software. Marketing departments have lead quotas and a variety of automation tools. Product teams, meanwhile, have had to rely on their instincts.

But this is changing. Systems of record, composed of elements like user analytics, in-app guidance, personalization, and customer feedback, are beginning to emerge for product teams. Data from the product team's system of record can now be warehoused with other company data, and then visualized alongside sales, marketing, and finance data, elevating the stature of product leadership to the executive level.

## WHY BECOME PRODUCT-LED?

One mistake people make is conflating the idea of product-led companies with "product-led growth," or PLG, which is really just

---

[3]Source: IDC Worldwide Semiannual IT Spending Guide: Line of Business, 2016
[4]Blake Bartlett, "What is Product Led Growth? How to Build a Software Company in the End User Era," OpenView Partners, August 6, 2019; https://openviewpartners.com/blog/what-is-product-led-growth/

a byproduct of becoming a product-led organization. PLG is using your product (and your product data) to convert prospects, retain users, and expand customers. But when we talk about becoming a product-led company, it's not just about changing how you build products; you are fundamentally rethinking the product journey. **It's a shift from thinking of your product as a thing you sell to a mindset where the product is a user's first moment of truth**. But to make this shift successfully, you need to transform your entire organization. Here are some benefits that you can expect to see from becoming product led:

## Greater Flexibility and Responsiveness

Most organizations say that they're flexible. Yet when it comes to building a product experience that fully engages customers, many companies still adhere to a static roadmap. Planning your company's product strategy quarters ahead may feel proactive, but what happens when users' needs change?

Product-led organizations can rewrite the roadmap when it needs to adapt. It's a shift from the past. Instead of working with known requirements, today's product-led approach requires you to run an endless series of experiments. That's because you can't base product decisions on what you perceive to matter, but rather on what user behavior, sentiment, and direct feedback say matters. These data points give a live view into the value your product is delivering and where it is falling short. Product-led teams also ask for input on their roadmap along the way and look for patterns in user requests. A product-led roadmap is a flexible roadmap. It adapts to the customer, picks up on both their explicit and implicit needs, and ensures that the product delivers exactly what they want.

## Faster Innovation

By investing heavily in customer support, many companies think that they can take care of all of their customers' needs. But even the best customer support is largely reactive, which means that it's often too late. In contrast, product-led organizations take a more proactive approach by pre-empting support requests altogether. As one report stated, 86 percent of consumers are willing to pay more for an upgraded experience, and 55 percent are willing to pay for a guaranteed good experience.[5]

That means that, instead of responding to customers after they've encountered a problem, product-led companies rely on usage data to help anticipate where in the product journey users are likely to get stuck. This additional visibility lets product-led companies either iterate their designs or use their customer success teams to steer their customers toward their objective. That's true responsiveness.

### Deliver Greater Value to Customers

Creating value for your customer is the core function of your product. Because it's historically been difficult for product leaders to quantify value, many report on transactional items, like the number of features shipped. But when you prioritize shipping features, you face unintended consequences like product complexity and bloat, which creates friction for your users.

A product-led strategy, on the other hand, reorients your organization around each step in the product journey. It does this by unifying R&D, sales, marketing, and customer success around product health metrics like feature adoption, breadth and depth of usage, stickiness, and customer satisfaction. Pair this with the aforementioned flexibility and responsiveness of a product-led organization, and you can start delivering immediate and enduring value to your customers.

### Drive Revenue and Retention Through Digital Adoption

In traditional organizations, it can take significant time and money to turn prospects into users and users into profitable customers.

---

[5] "50 Important Customer Experience Stats for Business Leaders," Huffington Post

Product-led companies streamline this process—all with an eye on retention.

Rather than having to rely solely on the persuasiveness of your sales and marketing teams, a product-led strategy allows you to use the product itself to drive growth. And product-led growth is hyper-efficient because it facilitates viral exposure, captures trial users, and provides a path to paid conversions—all within the product. As a result, product-led companies drive impressive financial results. One study reported that companies with best-in-class product and customer experience management practices recorded a 527 percent year-over-year customer profit margin spike compared to their peers.[6]

### Scaling Efficiently

It doesn't necessarily matter if your product is built on top of cutting-edge technology, offers first-of-its-kind features, or is fast or cheap. What matters is that it solves a real problem—and it does so in an enjoyable way. This is the cumulative and most important benefit of the product-led approach. You are transforming your organization so that it does not see the product as simply a vehicle for sales, but as a means to make your customers' lives better.

Successfully carrying out this mission means making your organization more flexible, responsive, communicative, and obsessed with constantly delivering value. Becoming product led is ultimately an aspirational mindset and approach to strategy, which is what makes it so beneficial: You are giving your customers the experience that they want, often without them even knowing that they wanted it.

## THE ATTRIBUTES OF A PRODUCT-LED COMPANY

Becoming product led is an ongoing process that should involve every part of an organization. To that end, here are five key attributes that every product-led organization should embody.

---

[6]Aberdeen and SAP

## Product Has a Voice

Product teams need to be more than just influential. They should have the formal authority to drive a company's roadmap, shape its business strategy, and set future goals. An effective way to do this is by giving "product" a seat at the table. A chief product officer can ensure that creating a valuable product experience remains the central concern and advantage of your business.

## Data-informed

Instinct and expertise were once all that product teams needed to rely on. But to become product led, companies must now get as close to their customers as possible. This means product teams should obsess over data. Moreover, you need to be willing to make changes based on data and to run experiments to collect data when it isn't available.

## Empathetic

Product-led organizations desire a deeper connection with their customer and user. They attempt to understand their problems, striving to anticipate what the customer wants.

## Collaborative

A product-led strategy is not something that one person or team can take on. It's an organization-wide effort powered by open communication and close collaboration. Across a company, teams should look for new opportunities to build bridges and contribute to the product. You should start by closely aligning your product and go-to-market teams, such as customer success, so that fewer barriers exist between what you're building and what customers want.

## Product Is the Customer Experience

Product-led companies must come to an important realization: The product is no longer just one part of the customer experience; it is the experience. Everything your organization does should lead back to it. Sales, marketing, service, support, and education must now converge both at the surface of the product and deep within the user experience. The product should communicate its value, teach its users, provide assistance, and more. In other words, efforts like selling to and educating customers that used to happen outside of the product are now part of the user experience inside the product. **The customer experience should become indistinguishable from the product experience itself.**

## TEAM COLLABORATION IN A PRODUCT-LED COMPANY

Successfully delivering a product-led experience to your users starts with common data, common language, and common definitions of success. This means that product-led organizations have a leg up when it comes to collaboration. After all, what could be a better unifying source of data, language, and success than the company's own product?

This is the essence of the product-led approach. Instead of keeping different departments separate, it encourages collaboration between every team by placing the product at the center of the business. Each team's goal, expressed as complementary KPIs, is to make sure that the product is delivering maximum value to the customer and the business alike.

For example, traditional companies may partition customer success and engineering, figuring there's little overlap between the two functions. But a product-led organization considers them two ends of a successful product experience. As the team closest to the customer, customer success can help engineering create a scalable product by keeping them aware of both short- and long-term needs. Engineering, meanwhile, can keep customer success informed of bug fixes, help them solve more technical customer challenges, and offer a better overall understanding of the product and its capabilities.

Similar opportunities exist for every team. By tying together each team with the common thread of the product, a product-led strategy promotes a much deeper level of cross-functional collaboration. This can help remove silos and reveal unexpected benefits for both the company and its customers. Adopting a product-led strategy fundamentally changes how individual teams function throughout your organization. Knowing how a product-led approach affects different roles is key to a successful transformation.

Here's what becoming product led will do to your customer success, marketing, and engineering teams:

## Customer Success

The rise of the subscription economy means that it has become easier than ever for customers to switch between vendors or even back out of contracts with few, if any, consequences. This has made customer retention an integral aspect of growth. And because growth begins with products that deliver ongoing value, remaining competitive increasingly depends on the presence of an effective and responsive customer success team.

This is why customer success represents the eyes, ears, and heart of a product-led organization. They live on the front lines, listening, watching, and helping customers find their way to value. And since a product-led strategy is based on a continuous dialogue with the customer, the success team does not have to depend on instinct and anecdote. They can measure and monitor customer health and happiness using hard data and then communicate customer needs to the entire company.

More than this, a product-led customer success team creates a close partnership between the company and the customer. This involves meeting them at every step of their journey, beginning with their earliest interactions and continuing throughout their relationship. Doing so not only positions this team at the front lines for customers, but also turns them into a pivotal link in the product feedback cycle. They can pair quantifiable usage data with customer feedback and stories, providing crucial context to the improvement process. This helps strengthen the link between customer success, product, and every other team, bringing the entire company into closer alignment.

## Marketing

Marketers could once create a compelling campaign to mask an underwhelming product. Not anymore. Social media, user-generated content, and easy access to information have tipped the scales. Users are savvier, and customers won't take you at your word. In place of a sales process, they want hard proof. As a result, the product needs to double as a sales and marketing tool.

Product-led organizations make product the star of the show. By insisting on a product that the customer will both need and love to use, and then introducing it through a free offer or self-service trial, they transform the product into its own vehicle for sales. They can further improve this experience with in-product guidance and communications that show customers around and encourage habits to form. This makes it possible for customers to discover the value of the product for themselves and on their own terms.

So, what do product-led marketers do if the product is essentially selling itself? They watch and learn, identify key activation points that drive usage and conversion, and use these insights to improve messaging and strategy within the product. This could include building a better onboarding experience for new users or helping them return to the product after a few days. As customers become hooked, product-led marketers use their understanding of usage and sentiment to identify power users and potential advocates hiding in plain sight. This turns the customer into a megaphone, helping to promote the story on the marketers' behalf. Growth becomes a natural part of the product experience.

## Engineering

Shipping new features can feel like a black hole for engineering teams. How widely are users adopting them? How useful are they? These are often frustratingly unanswerable questions, but not at a product-led organization. By continually measuring usage and talking with their customers, engineering teams can easily see how their efforts are paying off.

However, beyond questions of simple curiosity, knowing these answers has a practical use. As products mature and features proliferate, the cost and complexity of maintenance grows exponentially. Understanding product usage helps engineering teams identify parts of the product that they can consolidate or even retire. And, as the backlog of bugs compounds, understanding usage, sentiment, and revenue impact help development and QA teams prioritize their bug fixes. They can use their time to produce the highest yield for both the customer and the business.

Product-led organizations are also data-driven in how they roll out new features. Their engineering teams can begin with a controlled release behind a feature flag or an A/B test and then use this to assess uptake and sentiment within a narrow segment of users before releasing these features more broadly. And, as they adopt Agile and DevOps approaches that let them continuously deploy new features, they can work closely with product and customer success teams to develop in-product mechanisms that ensure customers find value with every change.

## WHO SHOULD READ THIS BOOK?

Becoming product led doesn't happen overnight. It requires intent, practice, and ongoing calibration. It is less a destination than a state you must deliberately maintain.

But neither is it an abstract goal. You are not simply trying to improve your product or become a market leader, both of which can feel ambiguous. You are putting in place a series of practices, behaviors, KPIs, and solutions that ensure that everyone in your organization is focused on the product as an engine of growth, retention, and expansion. This means that, although the process may vary by company and perhaps by industry, we can offer some actionable insights to help any organization along its journey to becoming product led.

There are a lot of books out there on product management and software development, yet little content is available on this growing operational challenge of building a product-led organization. You don't need a background in product management to get value from this book, but you should have an interest. This book will not teach you how to be a product manager (or UX professional). And this book is not intended for data scientists to extract deep algorithms on analyzing data. Instead, this book is meant as a practical guide for establishing a foundation of measurement, feedback, and continuous optimization in your product organization—in short, for becoming product led.

## WHAT DOES THIS BOOK COVER?

This book consists of three sections. In the first section, *Leveraging Data to Create a Great Product*, we'll dive into the notion that we can no longer afford to make critical product decisions on past history or gut instinct. We need to use data to inspire and inform our decisions. We'll talk about the kinds of things—both quantitative and qualitative—that you should be measuring and why, as well as how you turn that data into actionable insights.

In the second section, *Product Is the Center of the Customer Experience*, we'll discuss what it means to use your product to drive value for your customers. That begins with using your product to help drive awareness with potential users—all the way through how your product should be employed as an effective ally in converting users into paying customers. But when you put product at the center of the customer experience, you also need to expand the ways in which your product can take the lead in areas like onboarding, customer service, and building the kind of value proposition that leads to creating customers for life.

In the third and final section of the book, *A New Way of Delivering Product*, we'll show you how we need to look at how we design, deploy, and determine the kinds of features and products customers truly want, using the lessons we shared in the prior sections. We'll also dig into the dynamic art of product roadmapping and your role, as a product manager, in engaging your entire organization...as well as your customers, as you embark on your journey to drive growth by putting your customer at the center of the product experience.

In the pages that follow, I'll share lots of specific strategies and tactics that you can use to start taking action immediately. But think of this as more of a tactical guide than a playbook. My hope is that this guide becomes part of your reference library, something you pull out from time to time to get inspired and to put new ideas into action.

If you're reading this book, there's a good chance that we both share a passion for building great software products. I can't promise that I'll answer every question that you might have on the topic, but I'm genuinely hopeful that I will help to advance your efforts with a new way of thinking.

Let's get started.

# The
# product-led organization

# One

# Leveraging Data to Create a Great Product

Earlier in my career, I worked with a team that did an incredible job over nine months following a tight customer development process. They released this product to a strong positive response. It seemed that they had addressed a key customer pain point, which validated their hard work. Nearly everyone, including customers, sales, and analysts spoke highly of the product. I was proud of the team and felt good about our work. Yet, just six months later, we looked at the usage data for the product and discovered to our horror that few people were actually using it. Worse, the retention of new users who tried it was low. In other words, the product was essentially a failure.

I won't forget that feeling of surprise and disappointment anytime soon—or the lesson I learned. We had declared victory prematurely based on anecdotal evidence—not on clear quantitative measures. Applause and fanfare doesn't mean a product is great. We were using the wrong measure. We needed to measure what value our product actually delivered.

This lesson inspired the first section of this book, which focuses on the metrics you'll need to track to achieve your strategic, operational, and customer goals. In general, the challenge with metrics is that there is a nearly infinite set of possibilities to choose from. In order to select the right metrics, you need to start with this goal in mind—the Why.

# CHAPTER 1

# Start with the End in Mind

**S**tart with Why. This good advice was made popular by Simon Sinek in his best-selling book and now-famous TED Talk, "Start with Why: How Great Leaders Inspire Everyone to Take Action" (Portfolio, 2009). If you haven't seen Sinek's TED Talk, you may want to put this book down and start watching it now.

The second principle of the late Stephen Covey's famous *The 7 Habits of Highly Effective People* (Simon & Schuster, 1989) is to begin with the end in mind. What he meant was to set clear goals of what you hope to achieve so that you can both visualize what success looks like and know where you are on the path to that outcome.

At its core, the product manager's job is to connect the *why* with the *work*. While a simple story or sentence can be used to articulate "why," I prefer to have a bit more structure and discipline. When it comes to goal setting, I like to follow the SMART framework, which was first introduced in the early 1980s. SMART goals should be as follows:

1. **Specific**: What will be accomplished and what actions will you take?
2. **Measurable**: How will you get the data to know how you're progressing?
3. **Attainable**: Is the goal realistic? Don't sandbag, but also, don't set yourself up to fail.
4. **Relevant**: Does the goal ladder up to the strategic goals of the business?
5. **Time-bound**: Have you defined a timeframe for achieving the goal?

Violating this framework leads to dysfunction. There are a number of models that you can use to develop a SMART goal for your product. Let's start by discussing a few approaches that will help you better measure the strategic goals of your product as well as how those methods are a departure from more traditional metrics of success.

## SETTING STRATEGIC GOALS: MAKING A BUSINESS CASE

After I joined a company earlier in my career, they decided to enter a new market. The problem, however, was that they weren't getting any uptake from customers or other folks in the space—they lacked credibility. So, we made the decision to use the "Magic Quadrant" issued by the research firm Gartner as our guide. Every year, Gartner issued an analysis of the different competitors in the market and then awarded the highest rankings to those best positioned to serve the needs of customers. Thus, we took what Gartner defined as a market-leading position and used that to develop our roadmap. When we finished, Gartner placed us in a top position. As our product took off like wildfire, everything changed for us.

This is an example of manufacturing a business outcome. Our customers were large companies who treated Gartner's analysis as gospel. At the time, we were struggling to get on the map—and this was our way there. Gartner gave us the validation we needed. In many ways, this was a more efficient way to build our product as compared to, say, conducting a million surveys. We still needed to execute on the plan. It was stressful because this was still at a time when we shipped software in a box. We needed to get it right, which, fortunately, we did.

Here is another way to frame what we did with the Magic Quadrant—or: we executed on a business case, which is a great way to describe the why of any piece of work. Typically, people associate a "business case" with a long essay or burdensome process—for instance, a 100-slide PowerPoint deck developed by a management consulting firm—the sort of red meat for mockery that you might find in a Dilbert cartoon.

This doesn't have to be the case, however. Having a simple one-page business case is certainly a lot better than having nothing at all. In fact, sometimes it's even better. In the spirit of the famous adage often attributed to Mark Twain, "If I had more time, I would have written a shorter letter." A more focused business case often leads to sharper, more incisive thinking. Don't waste a lot of time on this phase, but also don't ignore it altogether. Be sure that you're answering a few key questions, such as the following:

## Who Is the Target Audience?

Who are you building your product or service for? What's their role in the value chain and the decision-making process? Is what you're building intended for users of the product or service? Is it intended for buyers? Or maybe you're building it for one group with the expectation of being paid by another group. For example, building a product for kids while their parents pay, or building for an audience while advertisers pay. In the B2B world, what sort of company are you targeting? What are their characteristics?

It's critical to document the "who" in the early stages of product development, or you could be measuring the wrong results. I often see walls decorated with "persona posters," which depict profiles meant to represent the types of people the company serves. Detailed and specific personas are intended to make the abstract "buyer" feel more real to the team that builds, markets, and sells a product. They literally put a face to the user and include enough information to enable the team to feel like they know the customer.

## What Pain Is It Addressing?

A product that doesn't solve a meaningful problem is probably destined for the dustbin. Rarely does a team commit resources to building a product without the belief that they're solving some need. However, the magnitude and frequency of the problem directly impacts the overall size of the opportunity. A common way to think about the value of the problem is to ask whether it requires an aspirin or a morphine drip. This is another way of asking: Is it a "must" have or "nice" to have?

You may notice that we started with "who" and "pain" first—I'm not suggesting that we focus on "solution." It's important that your goal or why isn't simply building something because someone asked or because someone else has it—you need to deeply understand the problem it's trying to solve for the audience toward which it's directed. In other words, taking orders from customers or following the conventions set by a competitor is not the path to innovation. Innovation comes from deep customer insight and empathy.

That's a challenge that many companies face, according to an analysis done by Christopher Condo of Forrester Research. As he wrote in a report titled, "Sync Developers with Business Needs":[1]

> [Today's] customers expect you to offer products and services as complete digital solutions that engage them via multiple touchpoints, including web, mobile, wearables, in-store, and in-car. But [application development and delivery teams] often lose their way as they strive to deliver these multifaceted applications because they don't have a clear view of the business objectives that their development efforts are meant to achieve...They are guessing at what features to prioritize.... Too often, they guess at what would be best, favoring "gut feeling" over a data-driven approach.

The key, therefore, is to use data and metrics to help identify and seek out what customers are really asking for.

## What Is the Desired Outcome?

It's also important to understand and document how this problem is being addressed today. If it's a problem that has been present for

---

[1]Christopher Condo, "Sync Developers With Business Needs," Forrester, December 19, 2019

a while (which is likely the case), people have found ways to work around it or solve it altogether. The solutions may be costly and not ideal, but it may be working for them, more or less—or not.

In my experience building software, there's nearly always an Excel spreadsheet lying around to address most every pain manually, albeit inelegantly. If the pain is known, there's likely some sort of solution in place. Your solution needs to be substantially better to be successful: that is, how much better is this solution than existing solutions? Ask yourself whether your solution is substantially better than the alternative, however inelegant it may be. Is it 2X better? 5X? 10X? How measurable is this desired result? If the pain is unknown, you have another challenge: that is, educating buyers on the presence, value, and consequences of ignoring a latent pain.

In the world of B2B software, there are generally three outcomes to target:

1. **Revenue**: How does your product help to increase revenue by affecting customer acquisition or retention?
2. **Cost**: How does your product reduce costs by adding new efficiencies?
3. **Risk**: How does your product help to mitigate business, economic, or market risks?

Let's talk through a few different approaches that you can consider when making a business case of your own.

## SHOW ME THE MONEY

For me, the revenue part of the business case is most important. This is the most common desired result, particularly in a robust economy (when the economy softens, the pendulum often swings to cost). Of course, this is fairly abstract. Is this revenue from a brand-new product where demand already exists? Is this a new feature that's expected to make your current product more valuable or differentiated? Is it an upsell to existing customers, or is it targeting new "lands"? Is it increasing revenue by decreasing churn? Personally,

I don't like seeing "increase revenue" as the desired result of a new feature without elaboration. It's just too abstract to be meaningful. I prefer to have more details on how it's expected to increase revenue. Here are some contributors to increasing revenue:

**Improving competitive win/loss** Are you building something because you've identified that you are losing customers to a competitor specifically because of a capability (or set of capabilities)?

**Improved analyst ranking** As I shared before, there was a point when I prioritized work that I knew would propel my product into the upper quadrant of an analyst's grid. I have mixed feelings about whether this is a meaningful business goal now, even though it led to more revenue and helped my company.

Increased revenue is just one desired result. The desired result should ultimately tie back to the audience and their pain. Hopefully, you're building something because you want to address measurably some kind of substantial customer problem or issue. And hopefully, it also fulfills your strategic objectives.

In the past, I've asked product managers to prioritize their work based on revenue. This typically leads each product manager to identify the most common feature requests from the largest customers. Then, the sum total of those contracts gets "attributed" to the work. It's a fast way to get a large revenue number. The challenge is that every member of my team landed on unrealistically (or maybe realistically) large numbers. When all of the numbers are large, it's hard to decide what's most important. Moreover, these product managers weren't going to customers and asking them: If you have to choose just one new capability, which would it be?

Revenue isn't the only economic measure you might want to prioritize, however.

## A FRAMEWORK FOR ECONOMIC IMPACT

In Don Reinertsen's *Principles of Product Development Flow: Second Generation Lean Product Development* (Celeritas Publishing, 2009), he writes that everything you build should be associated with an economic impact. I've had the opportunity to meet Don, and I recall him saying that he had two lines of product managers at his desk: one for people who could point to economic impact and one for people who couldn't. Which one do you think moved faster?

In larger organizations, how economic impact is calculated can become political, with each stakeholder vying for approval of their project based on the knowledge that resources are scarce. Let's just say that people aren't always grounded in reality in the assumptions they make in this area when bigger means better. This is why it's very important to develop a consistent company-wide framework to determine economic impact.

Reinertsen proposes "cost of delay" as a framework for making product development decisions. In essence, this model asks you to determine the economic impact of delaying the delivery of some product investment. In practice, of course, this can present itself in many different forms. Here are some ideas:

- Failure to ship a product/feature that you plan on selling yields a lost-revenue impact.
- Failure to ship a product/feature that a customer wants or needs could result in revenue churn.
- Failure to ship a product/feature that is intended to reduce costs or improve efficiency results in higher costs.
- Failure to ship a product/feature at a specific conference means a potential missed opportunity to capitalize on a source of demand, negatively affecting revenue.

Having used this framework for years, I realize that it's not realistic to come up with an exact dollar amount for every feature. Often, this level of analysis is only practically applicable at a very high level (for example, a new product or maybe a large epic). However, I have found that applying cost-of-delay thinking, even at the granular feature level, contributes to better decision-making. In these instances, I've employed models to approximate the cost of delay.

## SAFe

*SAFe (Scaled Agile Framework)* includes a model I've used often. The idea is simple: You specify a score for user/business value, time value, and opportunity enablement/risk reduction. *User/business value* is the measure of specific value that accrues to the user or business, respectively. This includes revenue, churn, and other financial outcomes. *Time value* factors in the timeliness of the work, including whether it is needed for a critical renewal, marketing event, or new regulation. For example, if you build tax software and need to support an updated tax code, the time value of this work is very high versus other items. *Opportunity enablement/risk reduction* measures the long-term impact and potential opportunities that the investment enables. This is an important factor when evaluating the value of fixing technical debt or building an API. For example, no user will ever ask you to fix technical debt, but if you don't address it, it may impact the quality of all future work.

These scores are all relative numbers. To use SAFe, you need to baseline the scores. Choose a representative piece of work that has a known and low value for the aforementioned areas and make that "1". Then, when evaluating new work, you and your team simply need to ask is this 2X, 3X, or 10X more than our baseline. Tally up the scores, and you get a proxy for cost of delay or overall value score.

An extension of this factors in the cost of the work. Take the aggregate value score and divide by the effort of the work. Then you prioritize the "Weighted Shortest Job First" (https://www .scaledagileframework.com/wsjf/). This technique is good for identifying "low-hanging fruit." However, in my experience, this technique is rarely valuable for helping prioritize large bets. The cost component nearly always reduces the value score below other items.

## The 60-second Business Case

Jason Brett, a senior product manager, introduced an interesting model to help guide business decisions related to products. He calls it the "The 60-second Business Case."[2]

Jason's goal was to develop a framework to help facilitate rapid conversations inside an organization in order to help understand the

---

[2]Jason Brett, The Pragmatic Institute: https://www.pragmaticinstitute.com/resources/articles/the-60-second-business-case

impact of certain product decisions. As he writes: "The 60-second business case can be an incredibly powerful tool to get everyone in agreement and to prioritize efforts more efficiently and effectively."

The framework he developed is based on a series of key variables: strategic alignment, operational necessity, revenue, improving customer experience, innovation value, and lowering costs. The idea is for the organization to assign a weight to each of these different measures, as well as its product management priority, totaling 100 points.

Based on the variables in this framework, a product team could then assess whether an item has a "high," "medium," "low," or even "zero" ranking. For example, an item that ranks highly with strategic alignment would support the company mission and advances the vision for the product. A high ranking in revenue would convey that the product would generate meaningful revenue in its first year.

As Jason writes: "We've figured out a way to measure each of these business criteria and each can be supported very quickly in a conversation. In defending a specific product, feature, or initiative, you can walk through the spreadsheet and say something is important, because it's got high strategic alignment and here's how."

These rankings are, for the most part, mostly subjective based on a team's informed opinions. They can also shift over time as your organization's priorities evolve. Your goal may not be revenue or cost savings. It may be as simple as learning something new or gaining insight about markets or products. When launching something new, it's common to run experiments focused on delivering validated "learnings." This concept was made popular by *The Lean Startup: How Today's Entrepreneurs Use Continuous Innovation to Create Radically Successful Businesses*, by Eric Ries (Currency, 2011). The "why" is the learning you hope to gain via the experiment. We'll explore further how to run effective experiments in Chapter 3, "Turning Customer Data into Insights."

## Having a Product Point of View

Great products come to fruition when great product people have strong opinions about what makes their products different and special. I can think of no better example of this than Steve Jobs, probably the most opinionated product person of all time. It was he who said that computers didn't need keyboards ... or floppy disks and CDs. The products that Jobs and his team designed reflected his ethos. The way that people think about products has a dramatic impact on what they actually build, and the experience users and customers have with those products.

So, what's your point of view, and why will that connect with your customer? I believe product teams (and companies) should have a distinct point of view and not be afraid to go against the grain. For example, in the early days of Pendo, we set out to build a broad platform. This ran counter to conventional wisdom—startups were supposed to focus on one narrow thing and dominate it before moving on to something else. We were so unique at the time that a prospect described our solution as "ungainly." Of course, I didn't feel great about this description at the time, but now the breadth of our capabilities is becoming more of an industry standard.

These are just a couple of examples of product points of view (or opinions). Most great products are born out of a series of strong opinions. Teams should document the things that matter most to them and use them as a North Star as they cast vision and make decisions about their products.

## SETTING OPERATIONAL GOALS: THE GUARDRAILS AROUND YOUR PRODUCT

Once you've established a business case and goals, how do you know if you're doing a good job? How do you know that you made a change that results in a positive outcome—or a poor one? What do you report to the leadership team of your company on a weekly basis regarding this product? Here is where operational metrics become important.

Nearly every part of a business has operational metrics, which are well-known and agreed-upon standards that help gauge how your business is doing. Marketing has leads and pipeline as a tracking mechanism for sales prospects. Sales has revenue, attainment (how salespeople perform relative to their targets), and so forth. Finance has gross margin and cash burn.

Broadly, these operational metrics fall into the category of *Key Performance Indicators (KPIs)*. I like to think of KPIs as guard rails. With markets moving more quickly than ever, KPIs keep you on track and let you know when you might need to turn the steering wheel to keep you safe. Targets are a subset of KPIs and represent a value that you desire to achieve within a KPI. For example, you may have Net Promoter Score (NPS)—a topic we will discuss in more detail in Chapter 2, "You Are What You Measure"—as a KPI, which you hope to keep above 10. You report on it weekly, and you take action if it goes below 10. Or, you can set NPS at a target of 25. This means that you want to increase the current score, and you report regularly on your progress toward this target.

## Moving Beyond Shipping

There was a time when the primary operational goal was shipping. But that strategy is now a relic. Today, most software is delivered as a service, which means that shipping code is a normal part of your daily and weekly rhythm. You ship relatively small amounts of code all the time—sometimes daily—and that makes the moment feel a bit less celebratory.

That doesn't mean it's any less consequential. If you're like most modern companies, software is the engine of your business. It's how you innovate and differentiate. Shipping code is still magical and important, but the specific cause for your celebration needs to move downstream from the moment of delivery to the moments of adoption and delight. And what's the point of building software in the first place? Nothing less than driving adoption and creating delight. In the absence of these things, what have you actually achieved? Exactly nothing.

That's how your customers see it anyway. It's like the tree falling in the forest that nobody hears. Did it actually fall? Well, of course it did—literally. But is anyone the wiser for it? Nope.

Customer opinions matter more than ever, because in a SaaS world they can easily switch software, and your business depends on continuously renewing their loyalty. Take that for granted, and they'll silently defect.

That's why measuring what users do, how they feel, and what they want is so important for product teams. Without this insight, you're pretty much flying blind.

What customers do represents users' behavior inside your application. What features do they adopt? Which ones do they ignore? How do they complete tasks and journey through the app?

How customers feel represents users' sentiment based on their experience in your app. Where are they finding delight and frustration? What's useful and valuable, and what's annoying?

What customers want represents users' feedback and specific feature requests that help inform what you build and what you improve. This is the co-creation dialogue with the customer.

My company, Pendo, tracks user behavior inside of software applications to help product teams build the right things and improve the product experience. Every year, we aggregate and anonymize all of this data—some one trillion events across nearly 300 million users—to understand the state of software adoption by end users. What we find is nothing short of alarming.

Now we know that billions of dollars in R&D investments are wasted—practically set on fire—by publicly traded SaaS companies shipping features that customers rarely or never use. These neglected capabilities represent more than 80 percent of the features shipped by SaaS companies today.

Still, according to Pendo's annual "State of Product Leadership" surveys that we have conducted in the past, more than any other metric, product teams still measure their success on the basis of features shipped. As a colleague of mine likes to say, this is sort of like the CFO measuring their performance on the number of invoices paid. Declaring victory once a feature is shipped is also sort of missing the point. Fortunately, this dynamic is beginning to change.

Instead of treating this moment as the end of the journey, it should be seen as the beginning. This is where you shift your focus from building to driving adoption, learning, and optimizing.

This is why I'm such a wet blanket about the idea of celebrating feature releases—such celebrations give you false confidence, which lulls you into hazardous complacency. It fools you into believing that you're somehow done when you're only just beginning.

Peter Drucker famously said that you can't manage what you don't measure. This quote is now a cliché or a mantra, depending on your perspective. To me, it's just the truth. Measurement is at the heart of any systematic improvement made in business. Everything else is just dumb luck.

## Product Usage

*Product usage* is an entire class of product metrics. Goals range from how many users, to how often each user uses the product, to how long a person uses it. In many businesses, usage directly impacts business objectives. In B2C businesses that monetize via advertising, the number of eyeballs and amount of engagement matters—it's basically what you're selling to your advertisers. In B2B products, a lack of usage may reflect a lack of value that a user is getting in a product.

Our 2020 State of Product Leadership survey of 600 product managers found that product adoption and usage—more so than revenue—are the North Star KPIs for today's product teams. Ultimately, what product teams deliver is only as valuable as what's adopted by customers—and customers that adopt and regularly use products are the ones who tend to become loyalists and advocates.

The key is to set goals based on the behavior that most benefits your business. In some cases, it may be counterintuitive. For example, I've worked with a number of ad-tech companies that get paid based on ad impressions, not usage of their product. However, if it takes hours to create an ad, that slows down the creation of campaigns, which affects revenue. So, reducing the time required to complete an advertising campaign could be the right operational goal for an ad-tech product.

## Feature Adoption

*Feature adoption*, which measures the frequency of a user's interaction with a particular feature, is clearly a subset of usage. But it's more granular and indicative of behavior. Are users doing a specific thing? How often are they doing it? How many users? What type of users or customers are doing it?

The chart shown in Figure 1.1 highlights an example goal around a percentage of customers using a specific feature. The same chart includes several features for comparative purposes. Maybe you want the same percentage of customers to use a feature as another baseline feature?

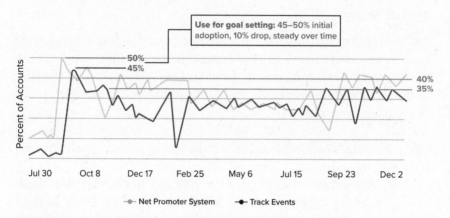

**FIGURE 1.1**   Graph showing new feature adoption rates by account
*Source:* Pendo

## Sentiment

How users or customers feel is a key operational metric. We'll introduce a number of possible metrics, but in general, *sentiment* is a qualitative measure that can be a gauge of product health. Typically, companies have goals to increase or maintain customer sentiment. We'll dive more deeply into measuring qualitative measures in Chapter 4, "How to Measure Feelings."

## Conversion

Nearly every software program or technology exists to help automate or accomplish some task or process. *Conversion*, at a basic level, is whether or not the user completes the task. Increasing the completion percentage (or conversion) is a key operational metric, and something we'll cover in more detail in Chapter 5, "Marketing in a Product-led World."

Many software systems have free trials. Converting a trial to a paying customer is an operational metric, and it is obviously a key one for a business.

### Retention

Given the effort to acquire customers, retaining customers and users is also a key operational metric. So defining metrics that reflect how many customers are renewing with you—as opposed to acquiring and converting new customers—can be critically important.

## GETTING CLOSE TO THE CUSTOMER

I grew up in Delaware, and, at the young age of 14, I started building software for a bank. I got the job in part because my mom had oversold my skills to one of our neighbors. I was a self-taught coder but passionate about software. I soaked up everything like a sponge. When the opportunity at the bank came up, I jumped at it. My job was to support internal bank managers by helping them automate tasks to improve business outcomes. It was a great experience learning how to combine technology with a heavy customer-first mindset. Unlike some of my peers, who never left their cubicles, I made time to talk to my customers and did whatever I could to help solve their problems. I developed the habit of listening and then asking questions as a way to learn what I could do to make them as successful as possible. That became a powerful "why" in how we decided to build things.

I continued to work for the bank even after I started college. When each semester ended, I would go back and help maintain the system that I had helped build. One summer, however, after I'd been there for about four years, the bank had a new IT manager with a very different mindset when it came to interacting with customers.

He told us not to listen to them; we were only to build what he told us to build. I remember thinking that this was strange. Wasn't it the customer's needs that mattered? It became clear very quickly that this new manager's approach was leading to poor results. So, I led a sort of coup where my fellow techies and I complained about the manager—and he eventually lost his job. Of course, on a human level that didn't feel great. But it was a validating experience for me—it proved that it really does matter what the customer wants. You can't build tech just for tech's sake.

When you walk a day in your customers' shoes, so to speak, you tend to be better at anticipating their needs. It forces you to understand their day-to-day challenges. This brings me to a huge misconception when it comes to market research. Too many people in the software world use Henry Ford's infamous quote (even considering the doubt as to whether or not he actually said it) as justification for keeping their customers at arm's length: "If I had asked people what they wanted, they would have said faster horses."

Modern-day examples are Steve Jobs and Elon Musk. Musk, for instance, claims he did no market research before his company, Tesla, launched the "Cybertruck" to much fanfare in 2019. But the fact that he developed a prototype targeted to the largest potential market for electric cars was no accident. Why was he touting the towing capacity of the truck if he wasn't convinced potential customers would care about that?

While he might not have brought four people into a room and asked them what they wanted in the Cybertruck, Elon understood what people wanted in any truck. The same goes for Steve Jobs. While he might not have conducted what we think of as "market research," he most certainly walked into stores in Palo Alto and watched how people used software. Biographer Walter Isaacson wrote that Jobs developed the iPod because it was something that Jobs himself wanted—which is actually just another form of market research. As a final example, consider that Mark Zuckerberg built Facebook after he was left out of the exclusive clubs at Harvard—he wanted to be part of a community that was accessible. Elon, Steve, and Mark suspected that they weren't the only ones yearning for a solution to a big problem. If you're trying to address pain that others feel, you'll have the empathy required to build a groundbreaking solution regardless of whether you send out a survey or host a focus group.

## What's Your Product's Job?

The late Harvard Business School professor Clayton Christensen popularized the notion of "Jobs to Be Done" in his seminal article, "Know Your Customers' 'Jobs to Be Done'" (*Harvard Business Review*, 2016). He subsequently presented a famous TED Talk on the topic, where he tells the story of a consulting engagement involving the McDonald's milkshake. The goal of the project? Find ways to reignite growth within the stagnant category of milkshakes.

The McDonald's milkshake project led to an inquiry into buyer motivation. Why do McDonald's customers buy milkshakes? What job do they hire the milkshake to perform? The team discovered that customers often buy a milkshake as a way to break up the monotony of a long commute. It was a subtle and unobvious conclusion that would never have occurred to brand marketers, who only thought of the milkshake as a frothy accompaniment to a meal. Understanding the job customers "hired" the milkshake to perform helped reframe the problem, allowing them to position and promote the product differently, which reinvigorated growth for the category.

The same Jobs to Be Done philosophy should apply to how you think about your product. By reframing your product in these terms, you shift the focus to an outside-in lens that emphasizes why customers are using your product. Ask yourself this: What are the jobs for which my customers hire my product? Better yet, ask your customers. And don't settle for superficial answers or conclusions that validate the status quo. Go find your own milkshake insight.

Once you understand the jobs that your product is expected to perform, you can deconstruct these jobs into the specific tasks in support of these jobs. And once you've identified these tasks, you can set goals and measure task completion—in support of these jobs—inside the product.

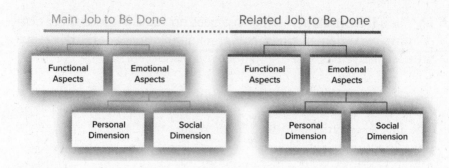

**FIGURE 1.2**   Jobs to Be Done (JTBD) Framework
*Source:* Pendo

Now let's use TurboTax®, Intuit's popular tax preparation software, as an example of how to apply this framework (see Figure 1.2):

1. **Main jobs to be done**: Describe the primary task the customer seeks to perform—in this case, completing their tax returns.
2. **Related jobs to be done**: Describe the jobs that customers want to complete in conjunction with the main job. For example, finding opportunities to reduce their overall tax burden.

Within each of these two types of jobs there are:

3. **Functional aspects**: This is the basic utility of what the product delivers—in this case, the tools to calculate and submit a tax return easily.
4. **Emotional aspects**: These are the feelings and perceptions elicited by the use of these functions. For example, the feeling that this tool makes you feel smart and capable by turning an otherwise painful process into a simple and intuitive experience while also finding ways to reduce your tax burden that you wouldn't have identified yourself.

These emotional aspects are then broken down into the following:

1. **Personal dimensions**: Reflect on how the customer feels about the solution. For example, are they appreciative of the convenience?

2. **Social dimensions**: This describes how customers believe others perceive them as a result of using the tool. For example, are they viewed as smart, capable, and resourceful?

Consider applying this framework to your product. Use it as a device for understanding what jobs customers are trying to get done and how you can best deliver on these needs.

## Employing Empathy Maps

Another tool available to product managers to help them better understand their customers is an *empathy map*, which is a way to visualize user attitudes and behaviors. By definition, an empathy map is a way to depict visually what we know about a particular type of user in a way that is not chronological or sequential. As illustrated in Figure 1.3, empathy maps are traditionally divided into four quadrants with the labels: "Says," "Thinks," "Does," and "Feels." Each quadrant then contains relevant information to that user.

- The **"Says"** quadrant will contain words the user said out loud during an interview or usability study. For example, it might feature a quote like, "I want something really reliable."
- The **"Think"** quadrant is related to the content in "Says" in that it reflects what users might be thinking—but also unwilling to say. An example might be: "Why can't I understand how this works?"
- The **"Does"** quadrant reflects direct actions that the user has taken—like how they navigate on the screen or get distracted.
- The fourth and final quadrant is where we reflect how a user **"Feels,"** which is where we want to capture elements like what worries the user or gets them excited.

It's important to recognize that an empathy map is a reflection of a human being, the different elements can be both complex and contradictory. You might also find that you lack information for a

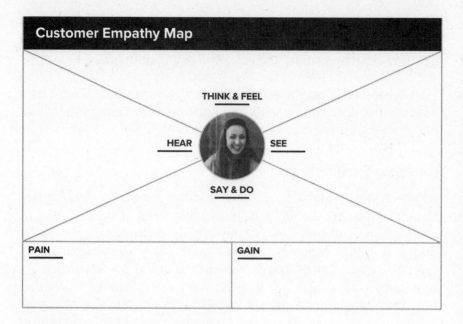

**FIGURE 1.3**   Sample Empathy Map
*Source:* Pendo

particular quadrant, which means that you haven't finished your research. This finding is valuable in its own right. The ultimate value of an empathy map is in helping a product manager uncover a new nugget of understanding about their user that they may have overlooked. That can apply to a single user as well as to a group of aggregated users. You can also have users fill out their own empathy maps, a strategy to help you learn about your users, and sometimes to help them realize needs they hadn't previously considered.

## Working Backwards at Amazon

Amazon founder Jeff Bezos has a famous process for new product development called "Working Backwards," in which product teams start any new project by writing a mock press release of the impact they hope that the future product might have on customers. They work backwards from that.

At a conference that my company hosted in 2019, Maiken Møller-Hansen, head of product of Amazon's Alexa Mobile, went deeper into this process, retelling the story behind Fire TV, which she helped to launch as principal product manager back in 2014. It all started with a question from Bezos: "What are we doing about over-the- air TV?"

While the answer at the time was "not much," Maiken's boss assured Bezos that her team had a concept in the works. Enter the Working Backwards process.

In most cases, Working Backwards was an exercise once Maiken's product team knew what they were going to build. But in this case, they hadn't spent much time thinking about it. It turns out that the exercise works just as well when the product vision is a bit fuzzy: Start with the customer and work backwards. Here are the steps that Maiken took:

### Immerse and Ideate

In Maiken's case, immersion means getting close to customers through a discovery process—she prefers the "Jobs-to-Be-Done framework" that we mentioned above. It means spending time with potential customers, especially the "super users," and understanding the jobs they want a streaming device to do for them and the unique value that Amazon could bring to their lives. According to Maiken, immersing yourself in the problem space and in the shoes of the superuser you're trying to serve can push the product or service to the extreme in ways an average user might not.

### Host an Initial "Hardcore" Brainstorming Session

Amazon starts by creating conditions that allow people to think and speak freely. This doesn't start with the disclaimer of "no bad ideas." In Maiken's experience, people don't want to put themselves out there—even with that in mind. Maiken aligns to Google's research around productive teams, working to create team psychological safety during brainstorming.

That's achieved by focusing the team on curiosity—learning and asking questions—rather than what it will take to execute on the vision. The outputs are key components of the Working Backwards document: a press release that helps to cast a vision for the product impact, as well as a series of FAQs.

### Create the Working Backwards Document

Maiken defines document in the very literal sense. Working Backwards documents are a six-page narrative memo. They start with a press release meant to capture the idea as customers might see it, using language they'd understand, visuals they'd get excited about, and questions they might ask.

Product teams brainstorm the headline they'd like to see atop the eventual announcement, the details that make this product unique from the competition, and a dream customer quote about the value of the new product or service.

### Perfect Your Idea Through Document Review

Relevant stakeholders then attend a document review, where they spend the first 20 to 30 minutes reading the document silently as a group. This ensures that everyone has time to read it and starts on the same page for discussion. Then they address three key questions to ensure the product vision is sound:

1. Do we all understand the product vision?
2. Can we improve on it?
3. Are we excited by it?

The answers to these questions help to inform updates to the document. The team then presents a final version to Bezos and other executives, after which work can begin.

The power of this process is evident at product launch, when a final press release is issued to the media. In the case of Fire TV, the product description and vision, even down to feature-level details, were strikingly similar to what was described in the mock version developed during the Working Backwards process.

## SUMMARY

As you embark on your product development journey, you need to begin by thinking of the end: What do you hope to accomplish with the product, and why does it make sense to invest the time and money? The first steps in answering questions like these are to define a mix of three different sets of goals—strategic, operational, and customer—that will help you determine if you're successful or not. Once you have your goals defined, you're ready to identify the different metrics that will help you measure your progress toward fulfilling your goals, which is the topic of the next chapter.

# CHAPTER 2

# You Are What You Measure

In the previous chapter, we discussed how to establish strategic, operational, and customer-related goals to track the success of your product. As Charles Phillips, now the chairman of software company Infor Inc., framed it in an interview with *The Wall Street Journal*: "One of the things my father taught me is: Do things that can be measured, because you can't rely on people liking you. You won't have the same access as maybe some other people, but if you can perform and demonstrate that you can perform, people will always take the next step with you."[1] In this chapter, we'll dive into the metrics that you can measure as you track toward fulfilling the goals you have for your product.

Early in my career, we hardly measured anything in terms of product. Revenue and defect counts were the key measures that we used. Don't get me wrong; revenue is a great measure (as discussed in the previous chapter), but it's lagging and not 100 percent controlled by the product team. A core reason for *not* having metrics years ago was that data was super hard to collect. Software had no pre-built way to send data back from the product, and you couldn't rely on any sort of network connection.

Fast forward to today, where many of the products that we build and use are hosted in the cloud. We can now access metrics in real time. Yet, I still encounter product leaders with a different mindset: "We know what our customers want—they tell us. We don't need to measure anything." Admittedly this mindset is becoming rarer and rarer, but it does still exist.

---

[1]Vanessa Fuhrmans, "Meet the CEO Trying to Make Business Software... Beautiful?" *The Wall Street Journal*, November 8, 2017; https://www.wsj.com/articles/meet-the-ceo-trying-to-make-business-software-beautiful-1510153201

As a result of the shifts we're seeing these days, you'd be hard-pressed to find a product manager who doesn't believe in the importance of collecting and analyzing product data. Being data-driven is no longer an exception or some fringe movement—it's the rule, the new normal. And the product leaders who can get the best product data and glean the most insights about their customers are the ones who will gain a competitive advantage.

A key to choosing metrics is having completeness, or ensuring there are no gaps in the data set you plan to collect. One of my favorite books on metrics is called *Measuring and Managing Performance in Organizations* (Dorset House, 1996) by Robert Austin. Robert was an advisor to one of my previous companies, and his research covered the misuse of data. He gives a great example about the dysfunction that comes when recruiters only measure interviews, rather than, say, the number of great new employees hired. The mistake becomes, therefore, that you focus on driving interviews for the sake of interviews, rather than finding great candidates (the ultimate goal). So be careful! Don't pick a metric that drives business outcomes misaligned with the business.

For modern product teams at product-led companies, the value is clear: Better measurement informs better experiences, and better experiences make for more successful customers. As a product leader, how do you know which data you should heed? And how do you figure out your product's key performance indicators (KPIs)? In this chapter, we'll explore some answers to these questions.

## STRATEGIC AND BUSINESS METRICS

Product managers typically don't like being measured on revenue because some feel that it's a metric they can't control. They don't own a marketing budget to drive inbound demand. They don't own a sales team (in a B2B environment example). Being held accountable for measures you don't control just isn't fair.

At the same time, measuring an output metric like delivery of features, which product teams can control, has potentially insidious side effects. "Where the metric goes, the effort will flow" is a good way to think about a common metric's dysfunction. When feature delivery is the performance metric, where will product teams focus their efforts? Shipping more features on a frequent basis, of course. The catch is that we lose focus on whether or not these features are useful to customers and aligned to the goals of the organization. You may say that this is an unfair indictment of people like product managers, who are generally passionate about customer value and business impact. To that I say: "Put your money where your mouth is."

It takes courage for product teams to hold themselves accountable to true business metrics. When they do, however, the quality of their conversations across the organization improves, and they earn influence and authority in shaping the direction of the company. These business metrics often include the following:

## Revenue or ARR or MRR

Revenue is the key driver of growth—and growth is highly valued. For any subscription-based business, there's nothing that matters quite as much as *annual recurring revenue (ARR)* or *monthly recurring revenue (MRR)*, which are the fees associated with access to your product. When handled correctly, ARR or MRR has the potential to be the gift that keeps on giving—an annuity that leads to a more predictable and profitable business. Securing this annuity, however, requires a differentiated product (on features and/or price) that proves its value during the contract term. A product that doesn't deliver on that promise is forever at risk of replacement.

## Conversion

Many self-service products have a free trial, or freemium, offering with an option to pay for premium services. The percentage of customers that optionally sign up to pay is typically called the *conversion*. While total ARR/MRR is the ultimate measure, it may be easier to measure the percentage conversion over time.

## CAC

*Customer Acquisition Cost (CAC)* is the amount it takes to acquire a customer. This is factored by totaling the marketing and sales spend required to land and convert the customer. Product-led companies typically focus on conversion to help drive down the CAC. In B2B or sales-oriented companies, product trials can also have a significant impact on the CAC.

## LTV

*Lifetime value (LTV)* is a measure of the future potential revenue associated with a customer, which is modeled based on retention and expansion assumptions. For example, a B2B company may multiply the initial transaction (the "land") by an expansion assumption (based on cross-selling additional products, or new lands in other departments or business units), then again by a multi-year relationship. Product teams can impact LTV by creating great initial product experiences that are sticky and have the potential to spread virally throughout an organization.

## NRR

*Net revenue retention (NRR)* is the percentage change in recurring revenue from your pool of customers. It is generally expected to yield a value north of 100 percent. NRR makes the assumption that you're going to lose a few customers, but you're going to find ways to expand the value of the relationships that you retain. To maximize NRR, product teams must keep a close eye on the causes of attrition and the leading indicators of expansion, making smart product and packaging decisions to drive down churn and increase expansion opportunities.

## Gross Margin

The *gross margin* is calculated by subtracting from revenue the cost of goods sold, (COGS), which for a software company includes, among other things, amortized R&D expenses and the costs associated with infrastructure and hosting if the product runs in the cloud. Product teams can help optimize gross margin by making efficient resourcing decisions (build vs. buy vs. partner) and investments that help minimize cloud hosting and data processing costs.

## Profitability

The *profitability* of a business is, of course, the calculation of total revenue minus expenses. Unlike gross margin, this also includes sales and marketing expenses. Product-led companies often reduce these expenses by offering affordable self-service packages that allows customers to adopt software in a low or no friction way (often independent of sales intervention) and provide mechanisms to convert and expand usage over time (again, often without sales intervention). Some of the most profitable companies in the world have effectively hacked their sales model by letting great products sell themselves.

## Win Rate

Think of your *win rate* as the yield on your product development and go-to-market investments. A higher yield means a better position. A lower one means you have work to do. Your strategy may be to improve your competitive position in the market. This could mean tracking the number of competitive encounters (which indicates that you're perceived as a credible competitor in a certain market) and percentage win rate. Of course, you can measure this in aggregate or against individual competitors. Typically, win rate is measured via data manually recorded by a sales team, so it is important to implement a process to ensure clean data.

## OPERATIONAL MEASURES

While the strategic and business metrics detailed above should be the true north for any company, they are in large part lagging indicators. They are important for measuring output and outcomes, but they don't allow you to make course corrections between reporting periods. Product teams need to measure and set goals around leading indicators. This means going a level deeper to identify the operational measures within your product that correlate with positive business outcomes. Here are a few measures to consider.

## Usage Over Time

The success of any SaaS application depends on retention, and retention depends on usage. This usage is often measured with a series of related metrics: *monthly active usage (MAU)*, *weekly active usage (WAU)*, and *daily active usage (DAU)*. As their names suggest, these are measures of active usage inside a product, and they are the most common ways to measure user engagement. But is more better than less? Often, but not always. Sometimes more engagement is an indicator of friction, suggesting that users are spending more time than they should completing tasks and workflows. Using these metrics requires that companies first define what active usage means for their specific product. For example, while a social network like Facebook closely monitors DAU, given that people don't typically travel daily, a service like Airbnb would attach a different KPI to product usage (see Figure 2.1).

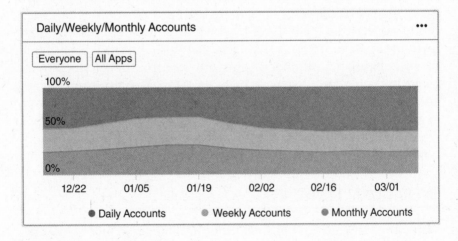

**FIGURE 2.1**   Usage Chart
*Source:* Pendo

## Stickiness

As a product leader, you're responsible for building a product that not only attracts new users, but one that also ensures they continue to re-engage with it over time. That's what the product *stickiness* metric is all about. When a product is sticky, users don't just sign up and log in episodically—they live inside the product. Users develop habits around it. Of course, the same principle applies as noted above; more usage doesn't always mean that users are getting more value. Nonetheless, the stickiness metric—depicted in Figure 2.2—is even more useful than other metrics because it homes in on habits forming inside your product by looking at daily usage as a percentage of monthly users. Said another way, stickiness is measured as a ratio of monthly users who come back daily. However, your ability to increase your score and understand what changes impact it is arguably more important than the absolute score itself.

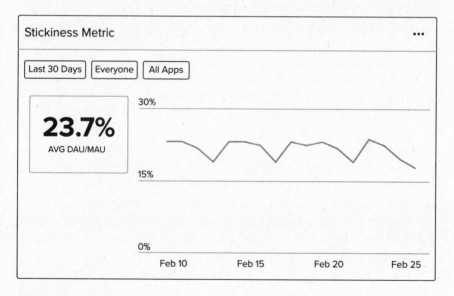

**FIGURE 2.2** Stickiness Chart
*Source:* Pendo

## Feature Adoption Rate

Every product team hopes (or even expects) that the features they ship will be adopted by customers. Sadly, that's not always the case. Let's recall that more than 80 percent of features are rarely or never used. When you consider the cost (and opportunity cost!) associated with these features, the business impact of this finding is staggering. That's why it's important to measure and set goals around *feature adoption rates*.

Examine the historical data in your analytics tool and compare adoption rates for your most recent launches. You should also look at feature retention rates 30 days following a launch to understand drop-off patterns better. Let's say that we recently looked back at two major feature launches and found that they had initial adoption rates of around 45 percent and 50 percent. Once our marketing campaigns cooled off, however, those rates dipped about 10 percent before stabilizing. That's the type of data that we like to gather before setting goals for future feature launches.

Persistence pays off when measuring feature adoption. For example, MemberClicks (https://www.memberclicks.com/), a company that provides membership and back office software for associations and chambers of commerce, released a new search feature and surveyed customers who had used it seven times. After each round of feedback, they would iterate on the feature, striving for continued improvement. Ultimately, users ranked the feature 4.6 on a 5-point scale.

Be sure to review feature adoption at the user level as well as the account level. While measuring feature adoption at the user level will allow you to understand the behavior of your target persona, measuring feature adoption at the account level (in other words, the company) will help you separate out those who may not have needed the offering because of their role (see Figure 2.3).

There is some good news to report. I mentioned that in our annual State of Product Leadership survey, product people often point to *features shipped* as the primary measure of performance.

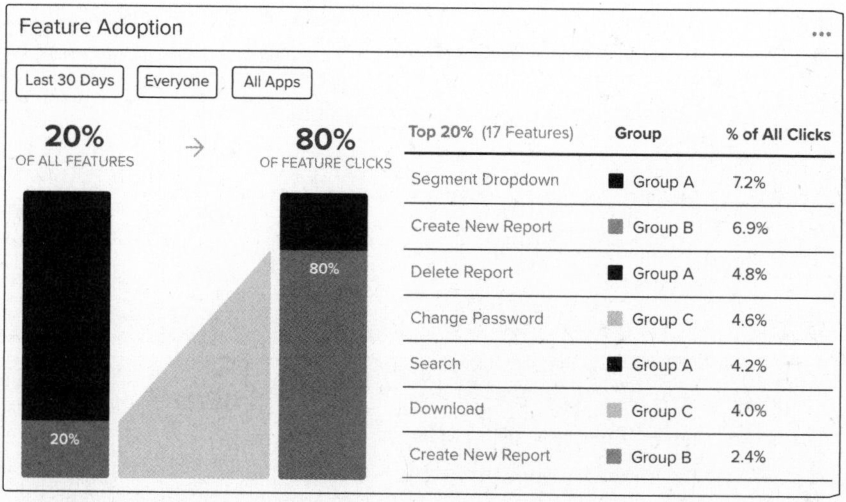

Feature Adoption                                              ...

| Last 30 Days | Everyone | All Apps |

**20%**
OF ALL FEATURES
→
**80%**
OF FEATURE CLICKS

| Top 20% (17 Features) | Group | % of All Clicks |
| --- | --- | --- |
| Segment Dropdown | ■ Group A | 7.2% |
| Create New Report | ■ Group B | 6.9% |
| Delete Report | ■ Group A | 4.8% |
| Change Password | ■ Group C | 4.6% |
| Search | ■ Group A | 4.2% |
| Download | ■ Group C | 4.0% |
| Create New Report | ■ Group B | 2.4% |

**FIGURE 2.3** Feature Adoption Charts
*Source:* Pendo

This has always pained us a bit, so we were encouraged to see the narrative change in the most recent iteration of the survey. It appears product leaders are getting the message. Today, more than any other metric, they look to *product adoption and usage* as the KPIs for measuring success. That's good news, indeed.

## Feature Retention

Becoming part of your users' daily lives rarely happens by accident. We've already discussed how product stickiness can help predict (and prevent) user and account churn. The same principle holds true at the feature level: By understanding which features keep your users returning, you can take specific actions to increase usage frequency. Ultimately, you want users to derive value from a broad set of your product's features. By monitoring *feature retention*, you can identify at-risk users and surface features that will help them become more successful (See Figure 2.4).

| Cohort Type | Cohort Size | Metric | Segment | Date Range |
|---|---|---|---|---|
| Visitors | 1 Month | All Activity | Everyone | Last 6 Months |

### Feature Retention

| COHORT | MONTH 0 | MONTH 1 | MONTH 2 | MONTH 3 | MONTH 4 | MONTH 5 | MONTH 6 |
|---|---|---|---|---|---|---|---|
| **Everyone** 14,043 Visitors | 100% | 32% | 23% | 17% | 10% | 5% | 1% |
| **August** 2,268 Visitors | 100% | 41% | 36% | 32% | 27% | 28% | 5% |
| **September** 2,339 Visitors | 100% | 41% | 34% | 31% | 29% | 4% | |
| **October** 2,595 Visitors | 100% | 36% | 30% | 30% | 4% | | |
| **November** 2,154 Visitors | 100% | 37% | 33% | 5% | | | |
| **December** 1,895 Visitors | 100% | 39% | 6% | | | | |
| **January** 2,791 Visitors | 100% | 4% | | | | | |

**FIGURE 2.4**   Feature Retention Chart
*Source:* Pendo

Vital product insights often surface when you compare feature retention across different segments. After all, different types of people and different types of companies will inevitably use your product somewhat differently. It is important to analyze those different segments (for example, free vs. paying, startups vs. enterprises, or individual contributor vs. executive) so that you can determine how their product behaviors differ.

## Breadth, Depth, and Frequency

At my company, we rely on three key indicators for measuring the health of our products' usage: breadth, depth, and frequency, as described in Table 2.1. Collectively, we call them "BDF."

**TABLE 2.1** Breadth, Depth, and Frequency Indicators

| Indicators | Definition | Measurement |
|---|---|---|
| Breadth | Number of people using the product for a given customer | Number of active users for a given customer within the last 30 days |
| Depth | Is the customer using key features that will make them "sticky"? | Usage of 5–8 key features that serve as leading indicators for retention |
| Frequency | How often do customers access the product? | Number of logins across all users for a given customer within the last 30 days |

*Source:* Pendo blog

By using the BDF framework, you'll be able to get a holistic assessment of your product's health. Moreover, by calculating a BDF score for each of your features, you'll be able to compare feature usage in an objective, insightful way.

## Product Performance

No one likes a slow product, and while performance metrics are typically engineering or DevOps measures, slow products lead to poor experiences.

## Product Defects

The quality of the product affects the experience. Products with lots of defects feel crappy. Often, I prefer to look at customer-reported defects, but just because a customer doesn't report something, doesn't mean they didn't see it (and that it possibly left an impression on them).

## Task Completion

Many products incorporate the notion of completing a task. Early in Pendo's history, we partnered with many "AdTech" firms. Creating and launching an advertising campaign is a complicated multi-step process, something called a *funnel* (more on those in Chapter 8, "Delivering Value"). We learned we needed to measure our own success by our ability to help customers complete tasks. By understanding where typical failures occur and addressing them, we could improve the rate of completion.

## QUALITATIVE METRICS

To achieve a more complete and accurate picture of user trends inside your product, you'll want to complement the quantitative measures of user behavior with more qualitative measures of user sentiment. This combination of qualitative and quantitative completes the circle of user insight, revealing both what users do inside your product and how they feel about your product. (The third leg of this stool is what users want, which we'll cover in the third section of this book). Following are some of the more common sentiment measures for product teams.

### Likert Scale

A commonly used survey approach is the *Likert Scale*, named after psychologist Rensis Likert. You've probably answered many questions using the Likert Scale. Likert responses can vary in length but are most commonly a five-point equidistant scale.

For example: "This book has changed the way I think about designing, building, and evolving software."

1. Strongly agree
2. Agree
3. Neither agree nor disagree
4. Disagree
5. Strongly disagree

### Net Promoter Score

For better or worse, *Net Promoter Score (NPS)*, which we briefly mentioned in Chapter 1, has emerged as the de facto product team standard for measuring sentiment. NPS is the methodology used by the Net Promoter System, first introduced by Fred Reichheld of Bain and Company in a 2003 *Harvard Business Review* article, "The One Number You Need to Grow." Subsequently, it became the topic of multiple best-selling business books. At the most basic level, NPS is a measure of a customer's willingness to advocate on behalf of a company or product. Reichheld's core premise was that if you get someone to put their reputation on the line in support of a product or brand, you could replace complex satisfaction surveys with one single question:

*How likely is it that you would recommend [product or brand] to a friend or colleague?* (See Figure 2.5).

According to the NPS methodology, 9s and 10s are considered promoters, 7s and 8s are passives, and 0 through 6 are detractors. An NPS score is calculated by taking the percentage of promoters and subtracting the percentage of detractors. Research by Bain and Company and others showed that focusing on that one question and number led to better business outcomes, namely retention and lifetime value. Today, many companies use NPS as a measure of customer loyalty.

By measuring NPS at the account level, you'll get a broad view of how willing your customers are to recommend your product. Then, by plotting account-level NPS against product usage and account size, you can unlock actionable insights into which customers may be at the highest risk of churn. You can also pinpoint the accounts where you don't have an NPS score and find alternative ways to gauge the sentiment of those accounts. The benefit of NPS is that you can now benchmark your score against others including those in your industry or segment.

Messaging customers as they use your product is also an effective way to increase response rates. Recruiting and applicant-tracking software provider SmartRecruiters (https://www.smart recruiters.com/), for example, had little idea how customers were using its product, so it replaced email surveys with an in-app NPS survey that it served to active users. This resulted in a 1,300 percent increase in participation, and the feedback helped SmartRecruiters identify long-term trends and improve its product.

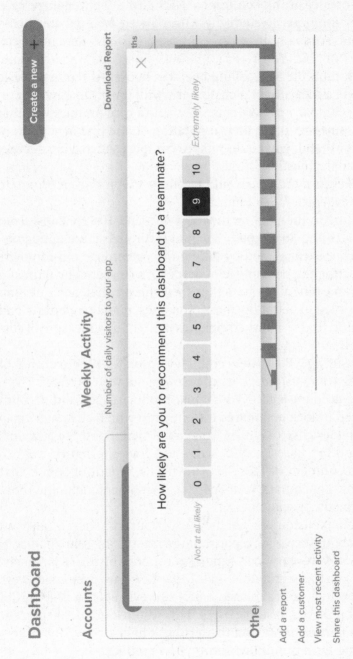

**FIGURE 2.5**  Example of an in-app NPS survey
*Source:* Pendo

User-level NPS allows you to get a sense of sentiment within your target persona. Since you designed your product for this very persona, expect user NPS scores to exceed account-level scores.

In order to get the most out of user-level NPS, be sure to include a section in your NPS survey that asks for written comments. These "verbatims" can provide valuable context for the numerical score.

Lastly, NPS is an excellent way to identify potential brand advocates. Savvy companies reach out to their promoters and ask for reviews or references; doubly savvy companies also reach out to their detractors to learn why they aren't delivering an ideal product experience.

Now don't get me wrong: NPS is not a silver bullet. If you ask me, the founding premise that this single question could replace all others was, and is, a bit flawed. Really understanding customer satisfaction, loyalty, and advocacy requires a constellation of different metrics. Some of these metrics are described below.

## Customer Satisfaction Score

The *Customer Satisfaction Score (CSAT)* is the most straightforward, on-the-nose measure of satisfaction, using a simple Likert Scale in the manner of the following question: *"Overall, how satisfied are you with this book?"* (See Figure 2.6).

## Customer Effort Score

The *Customer Effort Score* was introduced in 2010 by CEB, now part of Gartner, as a way to understand the relationship between effort and loyalty, and as a response to the exponential growth in digital

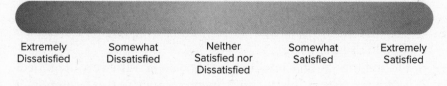

| Extremely Dissatisfied | Somewhat Dissatisfied | Neither Satisfied nor Dissatisfied | Somewhat Satisfied | Extremely Satisfied |

**FIGURE 2.6**   Customer Satisfaction Score
*Source:* Pendo

experiences that shape customer sentiment. CES is often used as a metric check on the user experience, especially for understanding a targeted area of the product. Think of CES as a transactional Likert Scale survey but focused on a specific experience. CES surveys typically employ a five-to-seven level Likert Scale, for example: "This chapter has made it easy to understand my options for measuring sentiment" (See Figure 2.7).

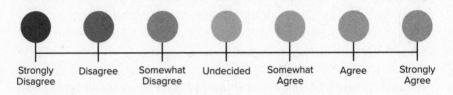

Strongly Disagree　Disagree　Somewhat Disagree　Undecided　Somewhat Agree　Agree　Strongly Agree

**FIGURE 2.7**　Customer Effort Score
*Source:* Pendo

## System Usability Score (SUS)

The *System Usability Score* was invented in 1986 by John Brooke as a way to assess the usability of your website quickly and easily with the help of your users.

The SUS is similar to the Likert Scale in that it asks users to answer a series of 10 questions by ranking how much they agree with the statement using a scale of 1 to 5, where 5 means that they completely agree and 1 means they completely disagree.

The following questions serve as a template, which can be customized to your own product or website:

1. I think that I would like to use this system frequently.
2. I found the system unnecessarily complex.
3. I thought the system was easy to use.
4. I think that I would need the support of a technical person to be able to use this system.
5. I found the various functions in this system were well integrated.
6. I thought there was too much inconsistency in this system.
7. I would imagine that most people would learn to use this system very quickly.

**8.** I found the system very cumbersome to use.
**9.** I felt very confident using the system.
**10.** I needed to learn a lot of things before I could get going with this system.

To calculate a Usability score, use the following formula:

*Subtract 1 from the score for odd-numbered questions, while subtracting 5 from even-numbered questions. Then add up the total score and multiple by 2.5. The result will be the Usability score out of a possible maximum score of 100.*

You can then use your score as a benchmark to assess your usability compared to your industry. The overall average score is 68, which you can use as a fast way to assess your own score and whether your usability is above, or below, average.

## Product/Market Fit Metric

A hot new email product called Superhuman (https://superhuman .com/) has generated lots of publicity for its amazing product experience. The founder, Rahul Vohra, published an insightful blog post on *Medium* about how they measured a leading indicator of product/market fit using a methodology that they borrowed from Sean Ellis, the head of growth at a number of high-growth software companies. They asked users: *"How would you feel if you could no longer use the product?"* They then rated the answers they received on a three-point scale—very disappointed, somewhat disappointed, and not disappointed at all. The idea, of course, is that the more disappointed a user would feel if they lost access to the product, the more connected they are to it. According to Ellis's methodology, 40 percent is the magic number for product/market fit. In other words, if 40 percent or more respondents say that they'd be very disappointed—Hooray! You've achieved product/market fit.

The key to this analysis, which is also instructive for other models, is segmenting the responses. For example, Superhuman learned early on that certain roles were not well suited for the product, meaning that they were unlikely to feel "very disappointed" if they could no longer use their product. The Superhuman product team wisely focused their efforts on the target personas that would be disappointed to lose the tool, which helped them drive stronger, more focused growth for the company.

## SUMMARY

In order to achieve the goals you've set out for your product, you need a set of metrics to measure accurately your progress toward attaining those goals. In this chapter, we've laid out some possibilities for strategic, operational, and customer-focused metrics that you can use to collect and measure the impact of your product. In the next chapter, we'll discuss how you can turn the data and information you've collected into actionable insights.

# CHAPTER 3

# Turning Customer Data into Insights

I just dumped a lot of metrics on you in the prior two chapters. I can imagine that you may be thinking, where do I even begin, and how can I glean insights from all these metrics? Well, obviously time series data is a good starting point that everyone should understand. Looking at any metric over time can uncover insights. You can also compare multiple time ranges to understand the impact of a change. The good news is that time series data is well known and understood, and it can help a lot. However, it doesn't offer a complete picture, and frankly it doesn't often provide enough detail to determine root cause.

There's an old trope that true innovators don't ask customers what they want because customers wouldn't know what they need—or they wouldn't have the words to describe it. Our data suggests that product managers buck this tradition, making decisions based on what customers explicitly request, more so than what the product managers presume they need.

Here are some other techniques that can be used (with or without time series data) to provide much deeper insights into customers, arming you with the right data to make informed product decisions.

## SEGMENTATION

*Segmentation* is the practice of sorting your customers by commonalities, like industry, size, location, persona, use case, or product use. Grouping customers by these various criteria will help you examine trends and set benchmarks. For example, your product team can use

**45**

these trends to understand the usage of customers who converted versus those who didn't, and use of such trends can inform future product decisions.

Segmentation is a really effective way to get insights into your customer audience sets. It's probably one of the most powerful ways to slice and dice your customer data. When you break people into smaller groups, you can learn a lot more about how to drive better results for them.

Your account managers can use these benchmarks to coach comparable customers on what actions in the product might drive a better outcome. Marketing teams can target segments of customers with personalized collateral and messaging. The goal is to create segments that are as homogenous as possible, increasing the likelihood that they will take the same actions with your product and have similar results.

So how do you decide on the right segments? Product management expert Roman Pichler says that you have two basic choices: segmenting by characteristics, such as stage of company, location, or industry, or segmenting by value, or how your product meets a certain need or job to be done. Pichler's suggestion? When you build or launch something new, segment first on value and then refine those segments by demographic or other customer commonalities.

A great example of the power of segmentation came during the early days just after Pendo launched. It involved a feature of our product that limited some users to read-only access to content. Most of us who used the product didn't have this feature option turned on—we had full edit rights, so we never really thought a lot about it. But when we conducted a Net Promoter Score analysis of our users, we segmented our customers so that we could see the scores of those who had the read-only feature compared to those who didn't. We soon learned that users with the read-only option rated us much lower than other users. In other words, by segmenting our users in this way, we identified a big problem that we didn't even know we had. Since we weren't using the product in that way, we didn't recognize that this was an area where we needed to focus.

Segmentation can be very useful for companies that offer free trials of their software. Analyzing how free users interact with your product's features differently than paid users could highlight ways to increase your conversion rate among your free users.

If you have B2B customers, segmenting your customers based on their size—small, medium, or large companies—can also shed a lot of light on the value you are (or aren't) delivering. For instance, if you're trying to move upmarket but you find that larger customers aren't using your product as much as small business customers, you now have a use case with which you can work to rectify that situation. Segmentation can also help you validate your strategy if you have introduced new features with which your primary target market seems especially happy. It can also help you identify areas in which to experiment.

## EXPERIMENTATION

Experimentation is not a novel idea. Most popular consumer applications—the likes of Google, Facebook, or Netflix—run experiments regularly. It is through experimentation that product management organizations are able to truly measure the impact of their development efforts on customer experience. Many business leaders lean on experimentation to measure funnel metrics, such as start-to-finish or quote-to-buy ratios. As Forrester analyst Christopher Condo framed it:

> Working with product teams, business leaders created a hypothesis about which features would resonate the most with their customers and at the same time satisfy a key business objective. These experiments ranged from small user interface modifications to larger changes like new workflows. In each case, this approach forced these teams to scale down the level of changes to a workable scope that could be delivered in a short amount of time, such as 90 days.[1]

---

[1] Christopher Condo, "Sync Developers With Business Needs," *Forrester*, January 6, 2020

One of the tools available to help teams organize and frame their experiments is called an "experiment canvas" (see Figure 3.1).

I have used a bunch of experiment canvases like the one shown in Figure 3.1 over the course of my career. They help clarify what you are trying to test and how you set up that test.

The idea, as we discussed back in Chapter 1, is to start with the end in mind. Create a hypothesis and answer questions like: "Who are you experimenting with or on?" or "Are you asking users if they want to opt into the experiment, or are you using a random sample?" It's really important when conducting an experiment to understand whether the results are statistically significant and to establish a confidence interval.

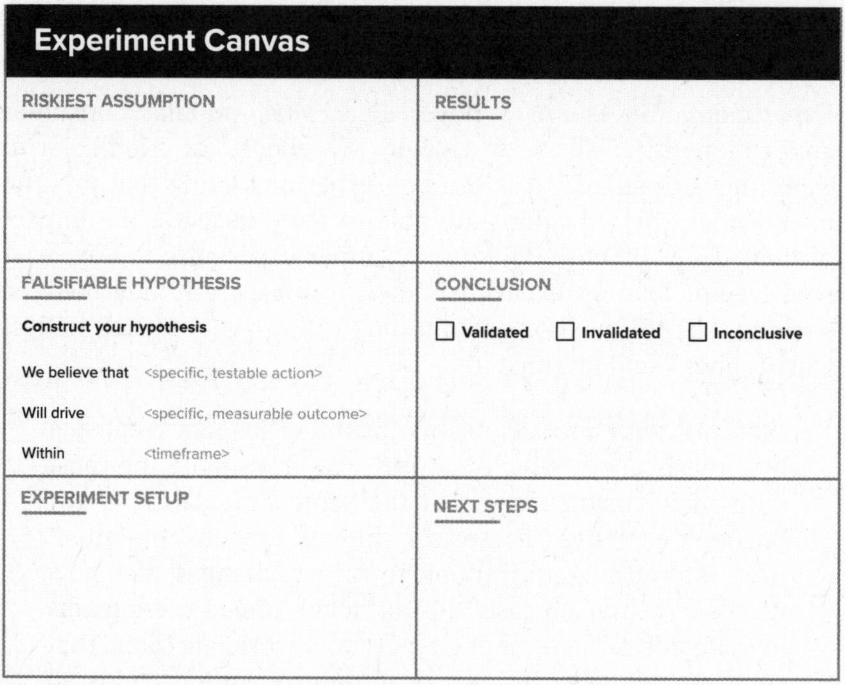

## Experiment Canvas

| RISKIEST ASSUMPTION | RESULTS |
|---|---|
| | |
| **FALSIFIABLE HYPOTHESIS** | **CONCLUSION** |
| Construct your hypothesis | ☐ Validated    ☐ Invalidated    ☐ Inconclusive |
| **We believe that**    &lt;specific, testable action&gt; | |
| **Will drive**    &lt;specific, measurable outcome&gt; | |
| **Within**    &lt;timeframe&gt; | |
| **EXPERIMENT SETUP** | **NEXT STEPS** |
| | |

**FIGURE 3.1** Experiment Canvas
*Source:* Pendo

Think about these factors in advance. Consider what conditions need to exist to validate—or invalidate—your assumptions. Then, perhaps just as importantly, decide what you're going to do next. Did you learn enough to double down in this area, or do you need to move on to another?

A classic example of an experiment we think about is an A/B test. These are super useful. This could be as simple as seeing which color button drives better usage of a page, or what text variant is better at guiding people to complete a workflow.

In an experiment enabled by the use of "feature flags," a topic we'll discuss in more detail in Chapter 12, "Launching and Driving Adoption," users are randomly assigned to treatment and control groups. The treatment group is given access to a feature; the control group is not. Product instrumentation captures metrics (or KPIs) for users, and a statistical engine measures any difference in metrics between treatment and control to determine if the feature caused—not just correlated with—a change in the team's metrics. The change in the team's metrics, or those of an unrelated team, could be good or bad, intended or unintended. Armed with this data, product and engineering teams can continue the release to more users, iterate on its functionality, or scrap the idea. Thus, only the valuable ideas survive.

To be effective, you need to be disciplined in how you run your experiments. A prime example is making sure that you have established a control group against whom you can measure results. I've seen some developers who will run an experiment on their entire user base. But when you do that, how can you be sure what exactly drove certain user actions?

Another element to be mindful of when you run experiments is ethics. I mentioned before that you might choose to allow users to opt into an experiment. Some users—especially B2B customers who are paying for your product—may be reluctant to serve as guinea pigs in your experiment. At the same time, other customers may relish the opportunity to serve as your development partner. The key is to be open with them up front and ask.

## COHORT ANALYSIS

Once you have your segments in place, you can begin to conduct *cohort analysis*. This is one of the key jobs of a product manager. Cohort analysis breaks segments down even further by grouping sets of users by common characteristics and then comparing the behavior and metrics of each cohort.

Cohorts might be segmented based on the first time they visit or log in to your application, or by the first time they use a certain feature. Cohort analysis allows you to compare the behavior of different cohorts over time in the hope of uncovering the characteristics of your most successful users and learning what activities are making them so successful.

Cohort analysis is a powerful tool in driving conversion activities. Marketers can discover if a certain campaign, channel, or page moved a casual visitor into a demo experience. Product team members can study which portion of that demo experience converted a prospect into a customer and then learn what parts of their product are driving engagement. Customer success teams can look at the highest and lowest performing cohorts of users to track customer health and, ultimately, retention.

Cohort analyses typically appear as a data visualization that shows how segments of users behave over time. As such, they have two axes with cohorts on one side and time range on the other (see Figure 3.2).

Cohort analysis tools typically allow you to build a report based on the following:

**Cohort type**: Users or accounts

**Cohort size**: Number of users or accounts grouped by a start date or action

**Customer attributes**: Size, business model, and type of plan

**User roles**: Function associated with the users

**Date range**: Cohort activity by week, month, quarter, or longer specific metrics

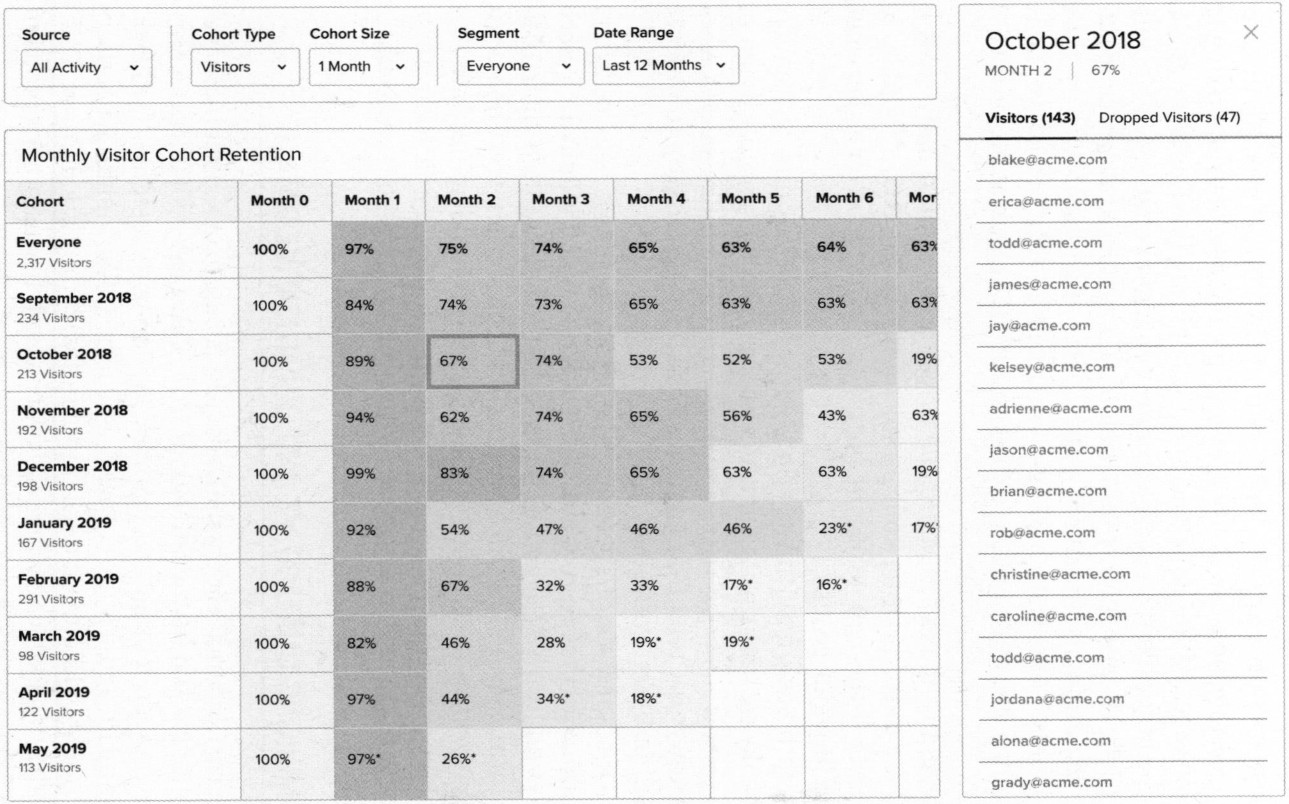

| Source | Cohort Type | Cohort Size | Segment | Date Range |
|---|---|---|---|---|
| All Activity ⌄ | Visitors ⌄ | 1 Month ⌄ | Everyone ⌄ | Last 12 Months ⌄ |

**Monthly Visitor Cohort Retention**

| Cohort | Month 0 | Month 1 | Month 2 | Month 3 | Month 4 | Month 5 | Month 6 | Mor |
|---|---|---|---|---|---|---|---|---|
| **Everyone** 2,317 Visitors | 100% | 97% | 75% | 74% | 65% | 63% | 64% | 63% |
| **September 2018** 234 Visitors | 100% | 84% | 74% | 73% | 65% | 63% | 63% | 63% |
| **October 2018** 213 Visitors | 100% | 89% | 67% | 74% | 53% | 52% | 53% | 19% |
| **November 2018** 192 Visitors | 100% | 94% | 62% | 74% | 65% | 56% | 43% | 63% |
| **December 2018** 198 Visitors | 100% | 99% | 83% | 74% | 65% | 63% | 63% | 19% |
| **January 2019** 167 Visitors | 100% | 92% | 54% | 47% | 46% | 46% | 23%* | 17% |
| **February 2019** 291 Visitors | 100% | 88% | 67% | 32% | 33% | 17%* | 16%* | |
| **March 2019** 98 Visitors | 100% | 82% | 46% | 28% | 19%* | 19%* | | |
| **April 2019** 122 Visitors | 100% | 97% | 44% | 34%* | 18%* | | | |
| **May 2019** 113 Visitors | 100% | 97%* | 26%* | | | | | |

**October 2018** ✕

MONTH 2 | 67%

**Visitors (143)**   Dropped Visitors (47)

blake@acme.com
erica@acme.com
todd@acme.com
james@acme.com
jay@acme.com
kelsey@acme.com
adrienne@acme.com
jason@acme.com
brian@acme.com
rob@acme.com
christine@acme.com
caroline@acme.com
todd@acme.com
jordana@acme.com
alona@acme.com
grady@acme.com

**FIGURE 3.2** Cohort Analysis Chart
*Source:* Pendo

Cohort analysis is also a valuable tool once you begin making changes to your application. If you made a broad product update, for example, you can study how specific cohorts are responding to the changes. If you targeted a specific cohort with a tooltip or guide, on the other hand, you can examine behavioral changes as a result.

Cohorts also give you a different way to go about conducting experiments. Breaking your cohort analysis down by time segments—like days, weeks, or months—can yield valuable insights. The key to making this effective is to look at the impact of an experiment or change in the product on the cohort. For example, it wouldn't make sense to analyze your cohort on a daily basis if you are only updating your product weekly. The goal should be to identify if the new group of people is having a better experience than previous groups.

With each new time period, you can analyze how the cohort is behaving and use that insight to see how the group's usage of the product changes over time. Cohort analysis is also part of what is known as "retention analytics," where you're trying to observe whether users "come back" to the product or not.

Of course, there are times when you might not have designed your product to retain users. The classic example would be a piece of tax software designed to give users the ability to file their 1040 tax form once a year. Once they perform that action, you don't want them to come back, right? Another example would be software that enables prospective students to submit a college application. Once they performed that task, there's no need for them to come back.

## COMBINING QUALITATIVE AND QUANTITATIVE DATA

The best product leaders make decisions based on a combination of qualitative and quantitative data. They combine insights from analyzing product usage and feature adoption with customer feedback, sentiment, and feature requests. The former illuminates what users are doing, while the latter illuminates why they are doing it. Only by studying both can you really understand the customer's problem and how your product can help them overcome it.

While you're probably familiar with using product analytics tools to capture quantitative data, understanding the surrounding context is equally as important. The best product leaders segment and prioritize feature requests based on a variety of factors, some of which can be observed through usage tracking, while others need to be collected in one-on-one conversations. It's also crucial to remember that data isn't a tool for removing human judgment, but a rudder for guiding decision-making.

*Qualitative data* include direct feedback from customers, including their specific feature requests and suggestions, their sentiment, and captured output from various customer interviews, interactions, and observations through user research and ethnographic studies.

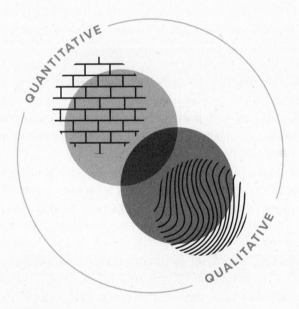

**FIGURE 3.3** When Qualitative Meets Quantitative
*Source:* Pendo

*Quantitative data* include behavioral data mined from usage of your products—which features customers use, which ones they ignore, where they get stuck and frustrated, and where they find value and delight inside your products. This also often includes financial data for understanding your customers' current and potential lifetime value so that you can make sound business decisions.

Something that we don't talk about enough when it comes to quantitative and qualitative data is how much they inform each other. The real power comes when you leverage both sets of data together. For example, you can use quantitative analysis to identify people from whom you then want to collect qualitative information.

Say you were analyzing your cohort analytics and saw that one third of your users dropped out after the third week of using your software. With that piece of quantitative insight, you can now reach out to those who dropped out and find out what went wrong. You can ask them questions like, "Why did you leave?" or "What happened?"

Qualitative insights typically don't scale well. There are only so many hours in the day where you can reach out and connect with users on the phone, take part in chat sessions, or even watch replay sessions (more on these below). You need quantitative insights to help direct your activity.

One obvious alternative to overcoming the scaling issue is to conduct random interviews or surveys. However, you could fall victim to selection bias because you might only hear from the loudest or most passionate customers, or even just the people who want to give you feedback.

Using quantitative data as your first step can also help you identify outliers—people doing things that other people aren't—which I've found to be incredibly valuable. In fact, I actively look for outliers—the people using the product in ways that really stick out. These are really good people to reach out to and learn from.

For example, I noticed that someone was using a feature of our product that few others even noticed. It was buried. And yet, when I drilled into the usage data, I learned that this one person used this feature some 3,600 times over the Christmas holiday. This became a really good opportunity to call this person and find out what they were trying to do. And, what could we do to make that job easier so they wouldn't have to do it nearly 4,000 times?

Insight like this is super valuable because it can identify how users might be misusing the product—or trying to solve a problem that we already built a solution for. These can be really insightful moments for improving usability.

When you find a customer who is using your product or a specific feature much more than anyone else, it also gives you the opportunity to ask questions like, should you charge them less—or even more? The point is that analyzing outliers both from a quantitative and qualitative perspective can provide you with great insights from which you might not otherwise benefit.

In our annual product manager survey, we asked about the types of data product teams collect on a continuum of quantitative insights that come from things you can count (adoption, usage, NPS score, and so forth) and qualitative insights such as feature requests and feedback. We were encouraged to see a near-perfect balance between qualitative and quantitative, which is exactly where product teams should be. Think of it as the combination of head and heart—a perfect union of the qualitative and quantitative that helps teams accumulate a fulsome view of the customer and a deep understanding of their needs. Similarly, the most valuable insights are often found at the intersection of what customers tell you explicitly and what they demonstrate through their behavior.

These insights should then inform personas and journey maps. Personas (see Figure 3.4) add a demographic and psychographic lens to your user segments so that you can design user experiences with a more informed understanding of your users' needs, wants, behaviors, and preferences.

Likewise, *journey maps* (see Figure 3.5) help you understand how these needs, wants, behaviors, and preferences change at the various touch points of the customer journey. Journey maps are particularly important for designing onboarding flows for new users because they explicitly call out how needs change across phases, and importantly, at transitions between phases.

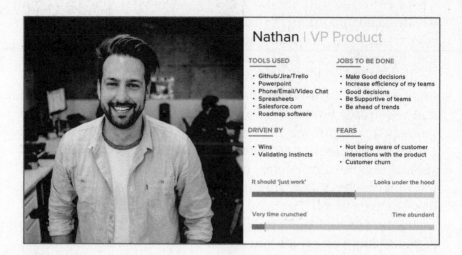

**FIGURE 3.4**    An Example of a Customer Persona
*Source:* Pendo

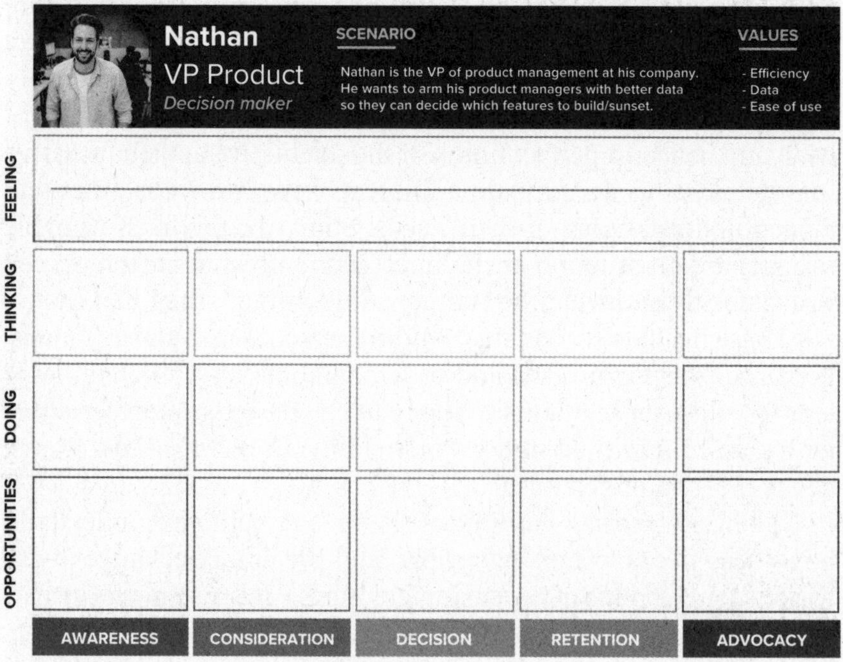

**FIGURE 3.5**    An Example of a Journey Map
*Source:* Pendo

It's important to recognize that your application is likely used by several different personas, each of whom is seeking to accomplish a different job inside your product and each of whom has their own unique preferences and needs. Onboarding (a topic that we'll explore in the next chapter) that's designed to be one-size-fits-all often becomes all-sizes-fit-none. Be sure to define personas and journey maps with the appropriate level of granularity—think of it as the Goldilocks principle of not too little and not too much—in order to capture the distinctions between these personas. By doing so, you're able to design onboarding experiences that match the specific needs and preferences of these individuals. In addition, by measuring user behaviors and sentiment over time, you can target additional support to help them find their way when they're stuck, or to convert a potential detractor.

## THE HUMAN SIDE OF SOFTWARE

I got some interesting insights from an interview that Eric Boduch, my co-founder at Pendo, conducted with Oji Udezue, the VP of product at Calendly, and, before that, the head of product at Atlassian. Udezue said that the biggest challenge in building software isn't the complicated code, the technical infrastructure, or the tough business problem—it's the people. Products are made by people, for people, so this makes sense. That's why product managers need to master the human side of software. Product managers are no longer expected to master code or have extensive domain expertise. Instead, they need to have great people skills. Udezue recommended that product managers be more intentional about building relationships with the influencers within their organization. It's even more important to build relationships with people who are skeptical about your product or team. Udezue isn't shy about having difficult conversations and says no product leader should be. Alignment is crucial to building a good product, so any disconnect is worth escalating. His team at Calendly constantly takes customer calls. He believes product teams need to be reminded that these calls are valuable. More importantly, they need to perpetually see that value. Most product teams assume that if they do customer calls for a quarter or so, they'll know everything they need to know. In reality, customer conversations should be continuous. Udezue is also passionate about asking the right questions and finding the right answers. However, he believes automation can be helpful in certain cases. Calendly automates generic customer calls so that every week, a PM is assigned a customer call. During these calls, they ask:

1. Tell me about a workflow that we're trying to optimize for you.
2. Tell me about a workflow that preceded that.
3. Now that we fulfilled all your hopes and dreams, what does your workflow look like?

From Udezue's perspective, this approach helps his team build better products and prepare for the future.

## HUMAN-COMPUTER INTERACTION

I went to college at Carnegie Mellon University in Pittsburgh, which had one of the first user experience, or UX, programs in the country. We used to put people in rooms with double-sided mirrors and then watch them perform different scenarios to observe if their behaviors matched our assumptions or if they did things we didn't anticipate.

During my sophomore year, one of our professors was working on a project to modernize the user interface for the Bloomberg terminals that Wall Street traders and investors used to make their transactions. The idea was to increase the productivity of those traders so they could capitalize on increased baud rates or execute trades in a fraction of a second. At the time, they were working to add a mouse to the terminal, which until then was all keyboard driven. The assumption was that the mouse would help make all of the information on the terminal easier to navigate. But when the new terminal was launched, productivity fell off a cliff. Suddenly, it was taking traders ten times longer to do their jobs. Why? It actually took them longer to use the mouse—they had memorized all the keystrokes on the old keyboard.

We had a similar experience at Pendo. To use the first version of our product, users had to know how to code using hypertext markup language or HTML. When we rolled out a new version, we replaced the need to code with the ability just to point and click. We thought that modern change would make it easier and faster to use. But the opposite happened. We actually slowed people down. We added more clicks, which made it less useful to them.

This kind of thing happens all the time—we assume that we are making things better, only to actually make them worse. Do you remember when Facebook introduced a new feature called Timeline that quickly bombed? People rejected it because it was different from what they were used to. They didn't see value in it.

My point is that you really need to watch someone using your product to get real insights into how you might help them do something faster. When you watch someone click and think out loud, you get feedback that you might not get when you simply measure outcomes. Sometimes those insights even lead to real innovation.

In order to collect this kind of information, product managers, designers, and UX researchers have defaulted to commissioning user testers, interviewing specific, cherry-picked users, or, in some cases, tapping hapless co-workers for help:

"Could you play with this new feature?"

"I want you to try this out. Follow these steps while I observe ..."

"What did you think about the new feature?"

Other approaches include surveys or feedback forms. No matter the approach, getting a qualitative pulse on user behavior has historically been error-prone, highly anecdotal, and terribly imprecise. Plus, because user feedback and testing is so expensive, it's typically limited in scope to a small sample.

Here's an example where quantitative data can improve these processes. Instead of commissioning random users or testers, you can measure who your most active (or "power") users are in a test. You can use data to target the opposite—brand-new novice users. You can isolate users or customers who consume different areas of your product or use your product in different ways. The point is that quantitative data informs who, and potentially what, to test.

Further advances in product analytics technology have made it possible to collect qualitative data about real user behavior at scale, with incredible precision, and without the bias. Using *session replay technology*, which you can compare to the game film that sports teams watch together to dissect their last match or to prepare for their next game, teams can capture the entire on-screen experiences of real users.

Using session replay technology, a designer can play back all user sessions in which a specific modal on a specific page was clicked. By watching actual users engage, hesitate, click, tap, and scroll, the abstract metric becomes real. A product manager can see when a feature is being used—or how often it is overlooked.

Replay technology grounds high-level quantitative analytics to real user experiences in an automated fashion.

## REPLAY IN ACTION

How is replay helping teams ground analytics to user behavior? The product team behind the popular business video platform Wistia (https://wistia.com/) noticed that users couldn't figure out how to upgrade to a paid offering despite the presence of a prominent blue banner pointing the way. Before replay technology, the Wistia product team had to brainstorm hypotheses and build tests based purely on hunches about what was amiss. By replaying session recordings showing users arriving at the subscription page with the intent to upgrade but ultimately failing, the product team observed the friction experienced by customers directly. With this critical qualitative research in hand, the team created a new, faster upgrade channel that quickly outperformed the old approach.

Relatively quickly, Wistia found that 60 percent of their upgrades were coming from their newly-created conversion channel—meaning that the majority of their upgrades were coming from changes informed by session replay.

In another instance, TravelPerk (https://www.travelperk.com/) used session replay to troubleshoot when a customer left a low NPS score. The team "went to the tape" and replayed the session that led to the NPS score. They watched in horror as the frustrated customer attempted to fill out a form unsuccessfully eight times. Further research revealed that more than a dozen other customers had tripped over the same bug. A quick help desk ticket submission later, and the critical issue was solved.

By connecting replay to existing quantitative analytics, it's never been easier for product managers to get the micro-answer to every macro-analytical problem that they encounter, which means better products and better customer experiences.

## SUMMARY

In this chapter, we discussed different techniques that you can use to turn the data and information you've collected from your customers into insights that you can leverage to continue to evolve your product. This continued the journey we started in the first two chapters of this section where we emphasized the importance of measuring goals and metrics as a way to ensure the viability of the product. In the next chapter, we'll dig into how we can measure more qualitative data like users' feelings.

# CHAPTER 4

# How to Measure Feelings

**W**hat should we build next? It's perhaps the most important question for product teams. It's also the hardest question to answer correctly and the most expensive one to get wrong. To be a product person is to live in a world of seemingly impossible tradeoffs, one where each choice has a high opportunity cost and confidence in each decision can feel imperfect at best. It's why, as humans, product managers tend to be relatively high on the confidence quotient. Anyone with a penchant to second-guess will probably find this an unhappy professional home.

Nonetheless, that's not to say that the average product manager is arrogant enough to trust their own instincts exclusively—at least one can hope, anyway. Besides, if we're being honest, it's not like they really have a choice in the matter. On average, publicly-traded cloud companies spend the equivalent of 21 percent of revenue annually on R&D. That's a large chunk of change to leave to chance.

While product teams are steadily gaining stature and authority in many companies, most still find themselves in the influence game. They're expected to craft persuasive data-driven arguments about how and where to place bets in a way that paints a vision for a future that feels compelling and real. In the absence of this data, decisions are biased disproportionately toward the HiPPO—the highest paid person's opinion. As Netscape co-founder and CEO Jim Barksdale reportedly once said: "If we have data, let's look at data. If all we have are opinions, let's go with mine."

Of course, it's not that product teams have been flying blind all this time. Surveys, focus groups, and customer interviews are all regular parts of their routine. But the effectiveness of these efforts are always in question. Customers aren't always the most reliable narrators. They either don't know what they want and need, or they struggle to put into words these things in a way that allows communication to happen.

This is not to say you shouldn't listen to your customers. It just means that you need to think about customer feedback as part of a constellation of inputs that you rely upon to shape product decisions—one that includes a blend of quantitative and qualitative insight. Moreover, when you ask for feedback, you do so in a way that positions you to dig deeper to understand the why behind their request and, importantly, to understand better the specific context, the relative authority, and the relative value of the customer who's asking you to trade one choice for another.

Feedback, as is often the case, is a bit of both art and science. The science is straightforward enough—asking the right questions at the right time, looking for patterns, weighing the feedback, and so forth. The art is using this feedback as part of a broader pastiche of collected insights that, together with expert opinion and the sort of ambient insight that comes from actual time spent with customers, renders the right narrative for your product strategy.

## MEASURING FEELINGS

At the risk of stating the obvious, how your customers feel about your product is something that you should take very seriously. Why? Because their expressed frustration is like the proverbial canary in the coalmine. It's a small, early qualitative indication that something may be very wrong.

The reality is that when you stop delighting your customers, they start looking for better alternatives and a company that's more willing to try just a little harder might win out. While quantitative insights are crucial for understanding which features are being used, how users journey through your application and where they're getting stuck or falling off, there's an equally important and highly complementary lens to consider: *sentiment.*

In product land, the definition of "sentiment" is as simple as it gets: "Sentiment is a view or attitude toward a situation or event; an opinion." In the context of your product, we can simplify this further: Do they or don't they like it? You can make reasonable guesses by observing their behavior, but it's often easier simply to ask, and asking has the added benefit of reminding customers that their voices are heard, and their opinions are valued.

Capturing sentiment requires careful consideration of *when*, *where* and *how* to ask:

## When

How frequently should you measure sentiment and when specifically on the customer journey? It's important to consider frequency to avoid survey fatigue and timing to ensure the highest volume of reliable responses.

## Where

Through which channels should you measure sentiment? In-product surveys and polls yield higher response rates, but email may help you reach users who aren't actively using your product. You want a balanced perspective from both audiences.

## How

Which questions should you ask? Net Promoter Score (NPS) surveys ask your customers how likely they are to refer your product. Customer effort score (CES) surveys ask how easy it was to accomplish a task. Different questions are useful for different reasons, and there is no one-size-fits-all method.

There's no single measure of customer sentiment. Ultimately, you'll want to experiment with a variety of different measures to best match what you're trying to understand. For product teams, NPS is perhaps the most common and widely adopted methodology.

# NAILING NPS

I distinctly remember when my team at a prior company used NPS to collect feedback from end users for the first time. The results were jarring. Before that, we would mainly interact with the designated buyers of the software—the people with whom we had relationships. With NPS, we could ask the people actually using the product what they thought—and what we learned was eye-opening. They didn't like the product much at all; we learned that we had a bunch of disgruntled users. It felt terrible to have users logging in each day to a product they didn't like to use. We clearly had many areas where we needed to improve.

As a product team, however, we were in such a better place knowing what they thought. We had visibility to our end users that we didn't have before and a new way to prioritize our work. It also lit a fire under us because we realized that if we didn't fix some things, we would greatly increase the chance of losing that customer—and maybe others as well.

To overcome that negative sentiment, we had to work harder to create a product that those users would recommend to others—we needed to earn that higher NPS score.

I saw a similar case at a company that provides software to dental offices around the country. This is software that dental hygienists—the folks that clean our teeth before the dentist comes in to perform their check-up—use to input new information into a patient record based on their most recent visit.

An initial NPS survey showed that hygienists hated using the software—it was really hard for them to use. But the decision to purchase the software was made by the dentist who owned the practice—someone who didn't actually use it. It wasn't until the hygienists were asked to give the software an NPS score that everyone learned how unhappy they were. That's why NPS is such a powerful indicator of what's going on inside a business.

While NPS may be the most popular measure of sentiment, it's hardly without its limitations—and its vocal critics. Jared Spool, another author and well-known UX consultant, has prosecuted his own Internet crusade against the use of NPS. If you ask me, his arguments, while intellectually sound, are missing the point. NPS alone is not the complete solution, and as Spool points out, the methodology has legitimate limitations. But show me one that doesn't.

What limitations? First, with NPS you're asking users if they "would" do something versus simply asking "Have you recommended XYZ product in the prior six months?" Intention to advocate isn't the same as evidence of advocacy. Also, advocacy does not equal loyalty. The fact that someone is willing to advocate doesn't necessarily mean that they'll buy, or continue to buy in the case that they're already a customer. Sometimes price, for example, becomes a real factor in purchasing or renewal decisions, and love for a product or brand doesn't always endure when budgets are tight.

Beyond these known quibbles, there's another fundamental (but often solvable) challenge with NPS: understanding *why* users feel the way they do about your product.

## Getting to the Why

One of the most conspicuous limitations of each of these survey methodologies is the fact that, to a greater or lesser degree, they don't reveal the root cause of positive or negative sentiment.

Generally speaking, there's a tradeoff between the broad applicability of a question and its actionability. For example, NPS is a broad question—how likely are you to recommend this product to a friend? But how actionable is the answer if you don't understand why? On the other hand, a metric like CES is more actionable but narrowly focused on just one part of the product. Finally, CSAT can be narrow or broad, depending on how you frame and target the question. For example, it could focus on a specific feature, the broader product, or on the customer's experience with the company itself.

Without other sources of complementary insight, none of these measures are perfectly suited for understanding both how customers feel and what exactly is causing them to feel that way. That's why it's so critical to connect qualitative and quantitative insights. By combining sentiment with product usage data, you can reveal a richer, more actionable picture.

## Don't Forget to Ask

While we're busy mining the data to make root cause inferences, sometimes we're inclined to ignore the more obvious step: asking the question. In addition to the numerical scale in an NPS survey, there's typically an optional follow-up question that invites users to sound off on the why behind their score. In practice, of course, it's rare to have 100 percent of respondents write in an answer. However, customizing the follow-up question based on the score helps to improve the completion rate. For example, imagine responding to detractors with the following:

> "Aww. we're sorry. What could we do better?"
>> While promoters might get:
> "Awesome. What do you like best about working with us?"

A contextual—and human—response will generally yield better response rates.

## Frequency of Program

When launching a NPS program, you need to decide when to ask the question. Knowing when is a function of asking why: What are you trying to achieve in asking the question? Remember that you only have so many tokens to cash in with customers. Use them wisely.

There are two basic styles of NPS: *transactional* and *relationship*. *Transactional NPS* measures the sentiment following an event, like a support interaction. Typically, this is used to judge an interaction with a company. *Relationship NPS*, on the other hand, is asked on a specified cadence. You'll choose how often you want to ask your users the question. This is a tradeoff between bothering your users and getting a more recent sense of sentiment. If you have a fast-moving product that you expect can lead to big swings in customer sentiment, you may want to survey more frequently. You can also choose who you want to survey, and this can have a major impact on the measures. Some B2B companies survey their buyers (whoever signs the purchase order) instead of the end users. This approach can be misleading because buyers may not yet have feedback from the end users, so it could give a false sense of security.

## Segmenting Responses

Another valuable analysis is to group NPS results by demographic, firmographic (if you're a B2B company), or even psychographic data (if you're a B2C company). For example, you might group data by company size or type for B2B organizations. In B2C organizations, you might group data by user role, gender, persona, or geography. It's possible that your product is resonating better or worse in particular segments. This could mean that you should either focus on the weaknesses or simply double down where you're strong.

Empathy maps can help here. They are a powerful tool that product teams can use to understand their customers and users better. In the prior chapters, we discussed measures of what the user is doing. We've yet to explore what they're saying in an attempt to understand what they could be thinking or feeling. What users say is a qualitative measure that can be aggregated and used to derive really powerful insights.

## FREE-FORM OPEN TEXT AND SENTIMENT ANALYSIS

The most basic type of qualitative survey is free-form text. Questions like "What could we do better?" or "What would you like to see?" will certainly generate some data and are a good place to start. Structuring the survey around free-form questions is the best way to maximize useful responses.

The challenge with free-form text is that it's hard to aggregate and trend. There are a couple of techniques that can help. There are a number of open-source systems for applying a sentiment score to a generic text input. This is an efficient method to process large amounts of free-form text. Typically, these systems will mark text as positive, neutral, or negative. Analyzing trends and changes in sentiment can be a simple proxy for improvement.

## Digging Deeper

There's great power in tapping into the voice of the customer in their own words, but collecting this feedback requires automation to glean real insights at scale. That's the role of *sentiment analysis*. There are a number of open-source systems for applying a sentiment score to a generic text input to help turn large amounts of words into the sort of insights that you can use to make decisions. Typically, these systems will mark text as positive, neutral, or negative, giving you an opportunity to slice and dice this data in order to understand the patterns and characteristics of positive and negative sentiment.

## Keyword Analysis

It's easy to process large amounts of unstructured or open text and find common words or phrases. While the most efficient method is to leverage an algorithm that can count keywords and phrases, it is common to support manual tagging, which is where a product manager would manually code the response to correspond to a more standard answer. Manual tagging is typically more accurate since a human is applying reason and context to categorize the free-form text into a common theme. In other words, it is taking a free-form answer and giving it some additional context. With advancements in machine learning, learning-based algorithms can leverage manual tagging as training data to marry the quality of manual tagging with the efficiency of automation.

## Word Clouds

Word clouds, like the one seen in Figure 4.1, are playful and fun visualizations and a form of keyword analysis. *Word clouds* plot the words most commonly associated with your product, with size or weighting proportionate to the frequency of the term's usage. Word clouds can be configured to remove filler words like "the" to focus on discovering the common source of the comments. There are plenty of free websites (https://www.wordclouds.com/) to generate them as well as libraries to embed them within products.

**FIGURE 4.1**  Sample Word Cloud
*Source:* Pendo

## Likert Scale

Another commonly used survey approach that we introduced back in Chapter 2 is the Likert Scale. Survey participants are presented with a statement: "This product is easy to use." Answers can be summed or averaged to generate a score. Surveys can include multiple Likert items or multiple statements and scales.

## COMBINING SENTIMENT WITH USAGE

While sentiment and usage are each individually valuable, the combination can be very powerful.

Imagine that you're trying to revamp a page in your product, and you want to collect feedback. So, you send out a survey to all of your users. You receive a number of responses ranging from "I love the current page" to "It's not valuable." The challenge with this approach is that it's hard to glean true insights. You'll likely have qualitative data from power users and novices in the same set. Power users develop habits when using software and might not recognize areas that would cause the novice and even average user to struggle.

But imagine that you had rich data on usage of this page and delivered different surveys to different segments of users:

**A survey to power users might ask**: "Hey, we know that you're super active on this page. What could make it better?"

**To occasional users**: "You rarely use this page. Why not? Is it not applicable?" This question can yield some interesting insights, especially if you understand the persona of the user. The page may be designed specifically for this persona, yet they don't get value from it.

**And to novice users**: "We're revamping this page in your product. You don't use the current version, but if there was one thing that we could add to get you engaged, what would it be?"

NPS can be combined with other quantitative data to deliver deeper insights. I've personally seen responses from users that are very negative and asked the question, "Do they even use our product?" Combining NPS with basic usage data provides much more insight. I don't need to ask users who don't use my product at all whether they would recommend it. Whether they would or not isn't incredibly relevant. Imagine if the person actually did recommend the product and, when asked "Why?" they had nothing to say. There is value in asking an infrequent user why they aren't using something they are recommending. However, if a person who uses my product regularly wouldn't recommend it, there are likely more valuable insights to glean.

## INCREASING YOUR SCORE

Getting negative feedback is a total downer. Each and every time I get a negative NPS response, I feel bad. It's stressful to pour your heart and soul into a product and *not* have happy users. My initial reaction when I get a negative score is to reach out to the user, hear the concern, and try to address it as quickly as possible. All of us want to convert every detractor into a promoter.

The challenge with this strategy is that it's hard. If you've dug a deep hole with a user, that hole may have been dug over a long duration of time. No single meeting or project will increase a person from a 3 to a 9. To improve your score, the first place to start is with neutral users. Increasing a score from 8 to 9 is much simpler and will result in a tangible improvement in scores.

## PERSONALIZATION BASED ON SENTIMENT

Imagine that you're using a product and you're actively frustrated and just informed the company. Wouldn't it be awesome if they treated you a little better because of this feedback?

This is an incredibly powerful and advanced opportunity to tailor the entire experience based on the sentiment of each user. Say a user provides qualitative feedback indicating areas of concern in your product. As you address the areas, asking for feedback and checking in to see if you've improved shows the user that you care and are actively addressing their needs.

Conversely, knowing a user is an advocate provides an opportunity to invest in the relationship. You can offer your advocates new features before others because they are a "forgiving" audience—they'll understand it's a work in progress and offer constructive feedback. And, they'll likely be honored to be the first to know.

## PRACTICING INCLUSIVITY

At one of the ProductCraft conferences we sponsor, we heard some powerful words from Benjamin Earl Evans, who had once been discriminated against by an Airbnb host because of the color of his skin. Benjamin, who now leads the anti-discrimination design team at Airbnb, posed this question to the audience: "How did our innovation do the opposite of what we intended?" Take a minute to think about that one.

Have you seen a human interacting with your product in a way that was opposite of what you intended? Or maybe they couldn't even use the product at all due to a disability that wasn't considered during the product development process. How can we be more intentional and thoughtful as we create experiences for all people?

Evans went on to acknowledge that we all have biases. Think about how damaging it can be if we build that bias into the products and services we design. He challenged the audience to think beyond the "average person" and to really consider how we might design for the future. For example, there are a billion people in the world with disabilities. So why are we still ignoring that population? He also made a great point that as we all age, we might experience our own disabilities at some point. Our designs should be timeless and universally accessible.

Accessibility isn't a new idea. In fact, this movement began decades ago. But while accessibility is required by law in physical spaces, it's not yet required in digital products. As product people—designers, product managers, and engineers—it's our responsibility to create accessible products and services for all.

Another lens is the toolkit that Evans's team created that gives designers a simple way to bake inclusive design into products and services from the beginning. The first step they've identified is to simply ask questions. These might include:

- Who might disagree with what I'm designing?
- Am I holding onto something that I need to let go of?
- What's here that I designed for me?
- What's here that I designed for other people?

Any product design team could ask themselves these simple questions and get started thinking about inclusivity. However, inclusive design requires self-awareness, advocacy, and community too. According to Evans, the three principles of inclusive design are growth, innovation, and belonging. He went on to explain each one in more detail.

**1.** Growth
Evans explained that for a company to grow, its leaders need to "own their lens." Your "lens" is the way you see the world.

One of Airbnb's main lenses was the English language. Because the company began in the United States, they ended up catering primarily to English speakers. However, this lens became more restrictive as the company expanded into the global market. By "owning their lens," Airbnb's leadership was able to recognize their own biases and address them.

2. Innovation

   In Evans' words, designers need to "champion the other" by thinking beyond the average person. What is the "average," anyway? To be truly accessible, designers need to create innovative solutions for those who don't reflect the frequently very narrow definition of the "typical" user.

3. Belonging

   According to Evans, product designers should constantly ask themselves, "Who are we missing?" Now, this may require changes in a company's internal culture and a rethinking of processes. A company that makes all users feel seen and accommodated can reap real rewards, both financially and in terms of customer satisfaction.

How can other companies adopt these principles? It comes down to practicing inclusivity. As Evans said, asking questions is a great place to start. Seek out resources from your users and from other organizations committed to inclusivity. Talk with your product management and engineering teams. Get everyone on board with the effort, and make it a priority. Realize that everyone has biases. Being aware is the first step to addressing them.

## CLOSING THE LOOP

Whenever you *ask* users what they think, the key and most important subsequent action is to demonstrate that you listened. The worst thing that you can do is ask for feedback and then ignore it. I find from time to time that teams can defend themselves or invent excuses for feedback that they neither expected nor felt like they deserved. Whether you like the feedback or not, treat it as a gift.

Someone took time to help make you better—this is a good thing. Be worried about the users who didn't respond—they are the ones who don't care as much and are flight risks.

The best way to demonstrate that you listened is to respond with as much specific detail as is feasible. An area of your product may be leading to some poor survey responses or even low NPS scores. In this response, *acknowledge* the issue and share your plan to address it. Maybe you are working on it now! If you can show prototypes of something new that addresses a customer's specific concern, show them. Be thankful and be specific. This is an opportunity to recognize someone who took time to give you candid feedback and make them a champion. Everyone likes feeling like they were listened to.

## SUMMARY

In this chapter, we learned about the importance of engaging with your users and finding ways to measure how they feel about your product. In the next section of the book, we'll discuss how to use what we've measured about our customers to place them at the center of the product experience.

# Product Is the Center of the Customer Experience

The biggest misconception in your journey to becoming a product-led organization is thinking that it's the product team's challenge; it's their responsibility or job. The product-led movement affects each and every facet and function of a company, and it should heavily influence your business strategy. Why? Because product-led organizations make their product the core of the overall customer experience. Whereas traditionally each function owned a piece of the customer experience, now consumers expect to be able to engage with your business 100 percent through the product. That starts before they even become a customer.

Let's take a look a typical customer lifecycle timeline:

**Top of the Funnel (TOFU)** The very first conversion activity happens when a person becomes a prospect. They engage with some piece of content, attend an event where your company is exhibiting, or hear about your services through word of mouth.

The best marketers can track a lead back to the moment when they entered the funnel, kicking off the data collection process.

**Demo/Trial** In today's try-before-you-buy world, most companies offer potential customers some sort of demo or trial experience. Once prospects have that initial engagement that got them into the funnel in the first place, your goal is to get them to try your product.

**Buy/Convert** A successful trial or demo comes down to the first impression. You've got to give these trial users enough functionality to prove ROI to their business and make them want to do more—but not so much that they never pay for your product and continue using the bare minimum of your offerings. That's bad for word of mouth too. We will talk in more detail about this in Chapter 7, "Getting Customers Off to a Fast Start Through Onboarding."

**Setup/Onboarding** The customer relationship changes dramatically once someone starts paying for your product. There are expectations that come with passing a vendor or service provider your credit card. There is excitement to get started too. Part of ensuring that your customer converts quickly from new and eager to happy and engaged is a quick process for installing the software.

**Activate** Your customer needs to have an early win to keep uncovering more of your product. Any expectations they had prior to buying should be met or exceeded—the faster, the better.

**Critical events** Your goal in the early stages of a new customer relationship is to get that customer doing the same thing over and over again. For example, setting up a dashboard and then engaging with it at some regular cadence, or downloading a report that becomes part of their company's metrics dashboard.

**Upsell/expand/renew** Once you prove that you can keep your customers engaged and happy, you can begin to find ways to provide additional value, and in turn generate more revenue for your company.

**Advocate** Customers who are enjoying or finding success with your product will naturally want to talk about it. There are many ways to harness that energy and enthusiasm to seek referrals and to fuel marketing campaigns and media pitches. Happy customers are your best marketers, and you should pull all of the levers possible to turn them into advocates for your business.

There is an additional conversion that you'll want to consider, and hope to avoid—*churn*. If a customer is not moving happily through the stages outlined above, you should consider that customer at risk and likely to stop using the product at the end of their contract. We'll discuss how to avoid that fate later in this book, especially in Chapter 10, "Renew and Expand: Creating Customers for Life."

We'll explore these different stages of the customer journey in this section of the book. As a first step, in the beginning chapter we'll walk you through how to build awareness for your product while also laying the groundwork for creating customers for life.

# CHAPTER 5

# Marketing in a Product-led World

Think about how you were introduced to Netflix. You were probably chatting with a colleague at work or with friends around a dinner table, and they mentioned this cool new television streaming service at a fraction of the cost of their cable bill. Perhaps you signed up for a month free and tried it out. After your 18th episode of *Friends* and hundreds of other shows at your disposal, $8.99 per month felt like a steal compared to your $100/month or more cable bill.

If you're still a Netflix subscriber, you've converted maybe dozens of times since then. It's up to Netflix to continue delivering shows and movies that you want to watch month after month, especially as you have increasingly more streaming choices. Go to the Netflix homepage and you won't see a typical marketing slogan or brand promise—you'll see an offer: "Try 30 days free." Netflix is betting that its product can deliver an experience so amazing that people will convert after that first month to a paid user. It doesn't even waste the energy or page space on marketing.

Netflix hits on several key trends that are making some of the largest software companies in the world so successful that it can be summed up with the phrase: *Product Is the New Marketing*. Said another way, many of the aspects that we traditionally associate with marketing, like encouraging users to leave reviews or share referrals, now happen inside the product.

## BUILDING AWARENESS THROUGH REVIEWS

Customers are smarter than ever before. Thanks to the proliferation of information that's now available on the Internet, paid advertising is becoming less effective at driving customer behaviors. What matters in a product-led world are reviews, which are how customers find and learn about your product.

Think about how Amazon and its reviews fundamentally changed how we buy things. We ignore things rated poorly, while highly reviewed items receive a disproportionately high number of eyeballs. If your product—whether it's a book, a knife, or an app—is featured in something like an editor's top-10 list, that becomes an incredibly valuable piece of marketing for your product. This drives activity in the top of the funnel, which is where your product gains exposure to new potential customers.

The mobile application market has felt this phenomenon acutely. So-called "App Store Optimization" (ASO), also known as "App Store Marketing" or "Mobile App SEO," is an entire discipline akin to Search Engine Optimization (SEO). Think about it. Just because you put an app up on the Google or Apple store doesn't mean that anyone will actually find it. So, just as you need to employ SEO for people to find your website as they search, you need to optimize elements of your app so that users can find it on a store. A few key elements to explore include the following:[1]

**App name, URL, and subtitle**: Does the name of your app connect to the kinds of search terms users might be using to find it?

**App keywords**: Just like with website SEO, put some careful thought into what keyword terms your users might be using to find your app.

**App ratings and reviews**: Users are drawn to products that have strong reviews. Not only that, they value new, fresh

---

[1]Lee Wilson, "A Complete Guide to App Store Optimization (ASO)," *Search Engine Journal*, March 14, 2018; https://www.searchenginejournal.com/app-store-optimization-how-to-guide/241967/#close

reviews, as well as the volume of reviews you receive. The more reviews, the better the chance you have of drawing in users.

**App downloads**: As with reviews, the more downloads you have, the more legitimate your app becomes to users. That's especially true when it comes to earning your app a spot in a store's own ranking lists of the most popular apps, which is yet another driver to drawing in new users.

As with SEO, you can't just "set it and forget it" when it comes to marketing your app. You need to be evaluating the results constantly, tweaking your keywords, and finding ways to drive more reviews and downloads of your app.

The impact of these massive shifts in how users find products online and on their phones cannot be underestimated. The experience that a user has with your product and how they share it with the world has completely changed how companies attract—or repel—new customers. Because reviews drive awareness of a product, designers need to be thinking ahead and anticipating what these reviews might say. If your product begins receiving negative reviews, you need to be paying attention and start addressing the issues, because that will immediately begin to influence whether new customers pay attention to your product or not.

This is just as true for B2B products. In the past, organizations building enterprise products would simply lobby (and pay) key influencers like analyst firms Gartner and Forrester to say good things about their products. Investing in building products that meet the criteria of an analyst firm to be positioned in the upper-right section of a quadrant was very common (and still happens in our industry). However, the introduction of crowd-sourced review sites like G2 (https://www.g2.com/) or TrustRadius (https://www.trustradius.com/) have changed the game. Now real customers are encouraged to share their software experiences unfiltered online. G2 even produces their own "quadrants" composed of real-life reviews from users. There is no way to game or control this position—you have to create a good product!

Nevertheless, even if you have the most beloved product in the world, you may still have limited reviews. This speaks to the importance of "designing in" prompts to leave a review inside your product. Product designers need to find ways to gently encourage really happy and engaged users to leave reviews. For example, when you ask someone to rate your product with a Net Promoter Score and they give you a high score, you can build in a function that automatically links your customer to a site where they can leave a review.

One example of this point is FourKites (https://www.fourkites .com/), a predictive analytics platform that connects to IoT devices and integrates with logistics systems to track shipments for Fortune 500 and third-party logistics companies, which encourage its users to leave reviews on G2. If a user responds to an NPS survey in their app, they get an email asking them to leave a review on G2. Using this strategy, FourKites has amassed more positive reviews than any of their competitors. The campaign has led to dozens of reviews with an average rating of 4.8 out of 5.

You can even build in language to encourage your users to leave reviews that might go something like, "If you have a few minutes, we'd love it if you could write a review about [product]." Or, "Calling all [product] enthusiasts! Share your experience in just a few minutes by writing a review."

You can also build in incentives for your users to leave those reviews. "Please write a review of [product]. As a thank you, we'll send you a $25 Amazon gift card. Start your review." Or, "Penny for your thoughts? How about 2,500? Write a review of [product] and get a $25 Amazon gift card."

It's important to monitor and measure how your review campaign is performing as well. How many reviews are you getting? Are there opportunities to tweak or optimize your audiences? Can you test different copy? How about offering an incentive, if you're not already? Again, the goal is to find ways to activate your users and customers to take action writing reviews, which will drive new users and customers to your product. If your product is providing value, and customers are confirming that with a high NPS response, it's the perfect time to drive these behaviors.

## REFERRALS

Another way to use your product to drive awareness is to foster and identify advocates. *Advocates* are brand and product ambassadors who can help proliferate adoption of your product. Typically, they advocate via referrals. There are actually two kinds of referrals that you can leverage: direct and indirect.

### Direct Referrals

*Direct referrals* are when you ask your current customers and users to, say, send a link to your product site to their friends and contacts. You might even attach some kind of award for that user to send the referral request.

One of the fun techniques we use at Pendo is an in-app guide to celebrate our users' anniversaries using the product. We throw virtual confetti and ask them what they liked best about the year. This is an opportunity to solicit feedback on the bright spots in the product as well as to create more advocates.

### Indirect Referrals

You can also get your product in front of new users in a more indirect way. Consider when you received an email from a friend and the bottom of the note says something like "Powered by Gmail." This is a powerful yet subtle way to advertise your product that drives virality while inviting a third party—whoever you sent the email to—to also explore using your product.

Zoom (https://zoom.us/) is a fantastic product-led business. If you aren't a customer/user, being invited to a Zoom call is the perfect referral. First, it's an indirect endorsement from the meeting's owner. They obviously use the product. But the experience itself is typically great, which is a fantastic way to "market" your solution.

## PRODUCT-QUALIFIED LEADS

A *lead* is an individual who may purchase your product. Some of those leads exhibit more intent to buy than others. Marketing often has programs and systems to score those leads based on their behavior. For example, attending a webinar shows a level of interest. But imagine that you have a person who has been to your website three times in a week and spent twenty minutes reading your pricing page. Do you think they are more or less likely to purchase than the webinar attendee? Marketing teams would deem both of these examples *Marketing Qualified Leads (MQL)* but would score them differently based on their behavior. Organizations leverage these scores to adjust their own behavior. For example, they might suggest a salesperson call the person who's looking at the website because they are more likely to pick up the phone and engage than a one-off webinar participant.

The simple truth is that pricing or a webinar aren't enough to get today's users to buy a new product. Regardless of whether they're considering a B2C or B2B product, they want to try before they buy (more on this in the next section). The key for product managers is to help make the initial experience and first impression so amazing that the user will ultimately pay for it.

That's where *product qualified leads (PQLs)* come in. PQLs are users that show interest in your product by signing up for a free trial or lower-tier paid version of your product. Or, to use another definition, PQLs are potential customers who have used a product and taken actions signifying a strong likelihood of becoming a paying customer. Companies that generate these kinds of leads have a leg up—they've already gotten the person into the product.

Consider the common strategy in retail or service businesses of offering discounts when a customer visits for the first time. A massage therapist, car wash, or restaurant is betting they'll win over that customer during the first experience and bring in hundreds of dollars of revenue over the course of that future customer relationship.

Product-led companies execute this strategy best when they immediately start analyzing how new users interact with their product and learn from their behavior with an eye toward converting them into a paid user. Metrics like the frequency of user logins, the features they use more than others, and the size of their user base reveal a lot about their potential as a customer.

This strategy, however, isn't solely for new customers—PQLs can also be existing customers who are ready to expand their relationship.

## TAKING ACTION ON PQLs

OK. So now we've covered how actual product usage can signal buying intent. What now? You could employ the same human-led techniques used to follow up on MQLs. This includes signaling these customers with calls, emails, and so on. Or, you can use the product itself to convert, upsell, and resell. We'll cover the latter in Chapter 6, "Converting Users into Customers."

## TRY BEFORE YOU BUY AND FREEMIUM

In a product-led world, people expect to try things before having to pay for them. It's a complete change in what customers expect. In fact, prospective customers may turn up their nose if you won't let them try something first. Furthermore, they do not want to be harassed by a human as they test something out.

One of the primary ways to let users try before they buy is what we now commonly call *freemium*. Also known as the "long tail," as popularized in Chris Anderson's book of the same name (Hyperion: 2006), a freemium offer gives users the ability to use at least some of your product for free in order to entice them to "convert" or buy the product. The goal, therefore, is to find a way to offer a trial version of your product for a limited amount of time—maybe 30 to 90 days—without requiring human interaction.

As you deploy a freemium strategy, though, it's important to remember the mantra that we shared back in Chapter 1: Start with the why as you set goals for freemium conversion. For many companies, the goal is to get as many people using the product as possible in order to build a reference set of users so that you spin the flywheel of momentum faster to become the product of choice. The more users you bring in, the faster your feedback cycle turns, which helps you build a strong product. There is a quote that has stuck with me that goes something like: "Big customers make you rich, but small customers make you great." What this means is that if you can please the small customers who demand so much, you'll have no problem satisfying the needs of the larger players. And one strategic way to bring more smaller customers into your orbit is by making it easy for them to try your product at a lesser cost.

There are a couple of different approaches that you can take as you design a freemium version of the product. You might give users the chance to use the entire product for free—for a limited time. Or, you might offer a light version of your product, with fewer features available, as a way to capture interest from a prospect. You might even provide a subset of features that are more of a commodity in the market. An example like Adobe Acrobat comes to mind. Adobe doesn't charge for its reader software. But they do charge for the software that allows users to create the content that they can then share via the reader. This is especially effective, because when users start sharing the reader with their customers, they're actually generating potential future leads for Adobe. This is product-led marketing in a nutshell.

There's another advantage to a freemium strategy—users often have different expectations for a free versus paid solution. We tend to be much more critical of solutions that we pay for than ones that we don't. Of course, this doesn't mean that you can create a crappy product or product experience—a bad or buggy product experience will hurt your freemium offering. However, free solutions can be a little more "do-it-yourself" than paid solutions. Open-source solutions are free and often target developers who like tinkering and don't mind having to set things up themselves. In the past, I set up a home file sharing system using custom hardware and open-source software. I enjoyed the setup and got a very powerful system very affordably. And I totally respected that I was the "tech support" when something went wrong with the system. In my business, I've purchased professional solutions, and for these, I expect the vendors to handle any and all issues.

Another great example of a successful freemium model is HubSpot (https://www.hubspot.com/). The company used to promote a free tool called Website Grader. Website owners could use the software to grade the accessibility and usability of their site. It would also offer recommendations on how to correct weaknesses on the site, which could be easily remedied by becoming a Hub-Spot subscriber. This was an ingenious approach to product-led marketing—they gave away a product that identified a need, which could then be met by the company's flagship product.

## Challenges with "Free"

While there is obvious power in using a freemium strategy, you also need to strike a very delicate balance in terms of what you give away—and what you don't. While it might seem obvious that you never want to give too much away, not giving enough can actually blow back on you. But fear of giving too much away is a powerful motivator. Think about a time when you've used a trial product—say, online media site—and the frustration you feel when a paywall comes up before you can even read the first page. I call this the "crippleware" trap. I become angry because I haven't even really gotten to try the product before I'm being asked to pay for it.

The key to avoiding this trap is to be very clear up front about what the user can expect to receive. *The New York Times* does a good job with its online edition. They tell me I can get 10 free articles a month. If I want to read more, I need to sign up for a subscription. This is the perfect amount of product for someone to trial before committing to buying a subscription. But if they gave me 20 free articles a month, I might never have the incentive to convert to a paying customer.

This is also a time to lean on your product usage analytics. The more you can track what your customers are using, the better you can find that balance point for your freemium strategy. Let's say your average customer creates five widgets on your site a month. Perhaps you set your freemium threshold at three free widgets—users need to subscribe to make any more. The idea is to find that pain point where they ache enough to want to buy the product but aren't irritated enough to walk away angry.

The moment of truth happens during the trial. Can the product deliver an experience worth paying for? And, can it continue to do that month after month? From the trial onward, most of the customer touchpoints are in the product itself.

## The Friction of Free

The status quo is a powerful anchor. If you've read Michael Lewis's *The Undoing Project* (W. W. Norton & Company, 2016) or studied heuristic biases, then you understand how much we hate losing something we already have. In fact, we typically feel the pain of loss as a multiple of the joy from an equivalent gain. That's why free trials work so well when they work.

In a scenario where the product's benefit is easy to experience and has few comparable substitutes, then a free trial is the best way to punctuate a fear of loss. That's because we don't want to lose what we actually use, so the magic of a free trial is less in its sense of lack of cost and more. The magic of a free trial is less about free and more about active utilization. In this sense, onboarding and marketing play an outsized role in making sure that the user realizes value early and often.

So, what could stand in the way of entrenchment? The primary culprit is the friction of opting in or the ease of opting out. Netflix has perfected the art of passive opt-in. During its early years of massive growth, when people got their movies through the mail on CDs, the Netflix streaming service was added as a free benefit when you bought its other products. Once the price of streaming went from $0 to $10, and then to $15 per month, it was still easy to cancel streaming. But it was treated as a feature and optimized against other user behaviors to take advantage of humans' inherent hesitation to opt out (but not in a way that was unfair or lacked transparency). But what if the feature set is complex or requires customization? Then we need a different framework.

## When Free Is Not the Issue

When it comes down to it, humans have short attention spans and can get confused easily. Just making something free of cost doesn't mean that it's actually free to the end user. Time is one of our most valuable commodities. Gaming and other social media companies understand that they are competing for your "free" time, which means that they have to make the product sticky and interesting to grab and keep the user's attention. Given that Facebook, Instagram, Snapchat, and other competitive services are all free, how do you get users to engage in your application? One example is Snapchat's feature called "streaks," where users get rewards for messaging each other over a number of consecutive days.[2] These streaks are now seen by teens as a measure of the quality of their friendship. Users are compelled to log in daily to keep their streaks alive.

### Case Study: Guided Test Drives

Like a lot of enterprise software companies, Catchpoint (https://www.catchpoint.com/), a digital experience monitoring platform that helps companies better understand the actual performance their end users are receiving in their products, offers prospective customers a 30-day trial of their product. "The way our marketing worked is that we'd use whitepapers and other assets to bring in prospects, and then work them into a trial," says Norm, a product manager. "The problem is that there's a lot of complexity and time involved with setting up the trial. We want to be able to demonstrate the value the customers

*(continued)*

---

[2]Taylor Lorenz, "Teens explain the world of Snapchat's addictive streaks, where friendships live or die," *Business Insider*, April 14, 2017; https://www.businessinsider.com/teens-explain-snapchat-streaks-why-theyre-so-addictive-and-important-to-friendships-2017-4

*(continued)*

can receive from our platform, but there's a lot of hand-holding required to get them there."

To get started in a trial, prospects have to sign an NDA, have a new client provisioned, figure out what features to enable, deploy the client, and begin tracking their applications. "Some of our users are really savvy about IT operations and networking, and they're able to get up and running in a couple days," says Norm. "But a lot of our users need help. There's a bit of a steep learning curve; there are a lot of bells and whistles in our application, a lot of things that you have to communicate. And that stuff is obviously difficult to do over the course of a sales call. We typically have several sessions where the account rep and a performance engineer will sit down with the client to show them what the tool is capable of doing."

It isn't just the sales and success teams that are involved in the trial. "There's engineering work involved in setting up a new client, and our finance team gets pulled in to set up the accounts and initial contract in our systems," says Norm. "It ends up being a lot of overhead for each trial, and it drags out the sales cycle. Our marketing team wanted to accelerate and simplify the process."

What Norm ended up doing, admittedly with the help of several of Pendo's features, was to create a short, guided self-service experience in the product. "The idea behind the guided experience was to eliminate as much of the setup as possible, while still being able to show the value of the product," says Norm. "We created a single client instance for the experience and filled it with dummy test data. Then we built a bunch of walk-throughs that take prospects through common use cases and showcase how they can get value from the application."

"Deciding which walk-throughs to include in the experience involved a pretty broad team," continues Norm. "Folks from our executive team, sales, and marketing got together and built a matrix of all the possible use cases and features we'd like to show. We prioritized the walk-throughs based on how well we could show the feature in the experience, which features are forward-looking—aligned with the direction the industry's going—and which ones address some of the most common problems our customers are trying to solve."

Norm's team then built out the highest priority walk-throughs as part of the guided experience. "We added each of the walk-throughs to the guide center," says Norm. "In some cases, where we couldn't illustrate the feature well—if it needed client data for example—we embedded screenshots or videos of what the experience would look like. We also integrated the guide center with Zendesk to make sure that users were well supported. From the guide center, a user can click to submit a ticket, open a chat session with one of our support reps, and, of course, opt into a full trial experience at any time if they like what they see."

## THE NEW TRIAL EXPERIENCE

The seven-day guided experience reduced both the trial time and amount of manual effort involved in trials. "We have marketing landing pages that allow users to register directly for the experience," says Norm. "Once they sign up, one of our sales development reps will add them to the experience. Our engineering team set up an API job that will wipe out their access in seven days. We integrated Pendo with Salesforce to make it easy for the sales team to track the progress of trial users. We run visitor reports to see which walk-throughs they're going to, which things they're checking out, what they're interested in, and push this info to Salesforce. At the end of the experience, the sales team can follow up with prospects and have a really fruitful discussion about the product and steer them towards a full 30-day trial.

"Users who have gone through the guided experience have a much higher baseline of knowledge going into a full trial, and as a result, are able to get much more value out of the experience," continues Norm. "Since launch, 10 percent of our marketing-sourced deals are coming through the guided test

*(continued)*

(*continued*)

drive and leads from the test drive experience close roughly twice as fast as leads that go through the full free trial process."

With the success of the guided experience, the team at Catchpoint is rolling out the content to all of their users. "We want to bring more in-app training to our paying customers as well," says Norm. "They'll have the same access to support resources directly in the product, the ability to open a ticket, or launch a chat with one of our team members."

## SUMMARY

Building awareness about your product begins by engaging users through your product. In a product-led world, marketing happens inside the product. That includes asking your customers to create reviews and share referrals to help build more awareness. And one of the best ways to engage new users is by finding ways to get them using the product through free trials and to let the product itself drive conversions. The ultimate goal, of course, is to find ways to hook your users by making them the center of the product experience. When you can do that, you'll increase your opportunities to turn those free users into paying customers. That's the topic of our next chapter.

# CHAPTER 6

# Converting Users into Customers

One of the interesting dynamics that's evolved in recent years is the advent of so-called do-it-yourself, or DIY, customer attitudes. In other words, customers love when companies give them more power to control their own outcomes. The good news is that we've already discussed a lot of tools that you can use to do this.

Here's one case in point from the product team at Citrix. They wanted to convert free trial users of its ShareFile® (https://www.sharefile.com/) file-sharing product to paid ones at a faster clip, so they set a goal of increasing their trial conversion rate by 10 percent. They wanted to get trial users to that "aha!" moment as quickly as possible.

The team conducted a *cohort analysis* of ShareFile users in order to understand the behaviors of trial users who converted the fastest. Then, they developed *product walk-throughs* to drive trial users to that optimal trial usage pattern (more on what these are and how they work coming up later in the chapter). They also used *product usage data* to learn what content was most effective in driving behavior and doubled down on it.

The Citrix team exceeded their goal with a 28 percent conversion rate, which helped drive an increase in revenue over the next year. By using insights from product usage data, Citrix showed users exactly what to do to have a successful trial and convert it to a paid user.

A key lesson the team learned came during onboarding: If you show users exactly what it is they want to do in the fastest, simplest way possible, users will find value and stick around. Here are some ways that you can measure and optimize conversions:

1. Track product usage to understand the behavior of users who convert better. By beginning to track the point at which prospects or customers convert, and how often, you can identify opportunities to improve the experience or insert messages or tooltips to help the right user discover new opportunities.
2. Set benchmarks for customer health. This likely includes some combination of feature adoption, feature retention, and NPS.
3. Determine the leading indicators of conversion, renewal, and expansion.
4. Develop a playbook for in-app messaging, including custom messages.
5. Measure what content works and what doesn't.

## CONVERTING PROSPECTS INTO CUSTOMERS

As we mentioned earlier, a big part of the "why" in offering a free trial product is to eventually convert those users and PQLs into paying customers. And, in a product-led world, you should be using your product to help drive those conversions. With the help of the data and metrics, you shouldn't rely on any one-size-fits-all approach to encouraging your customers to convert. Here are a few approaches that you might take.

### Usage Limit

Go back to the *New York Times* example I shared earlier. Once I begin to near my 10-article limit for the month, that might trigger the site to send me a personalized note that encourages me to sign up for a subscription. For instance, a note might go something like: "Hi Todd, it looks like you're enjoying reading our paper. Unfortunately, you only have one free article left to read this month. You can upgrade to a full subscription, and we'll even give you the first month free!" While this works for the *Times*, it's important to understand your market. If they have a clear alternative, you could run the risk of alienating your users and sending them to a competitor if your action is too abrupt or irritating. To this point, it's important to warn the users in advance if a trial is ending. The *Times* tells you how many articles you have left each time you read one. You know what you're signing up for, and there's no surprise when you reach the limit.

## Heavy Usage

Another potential product-led trigger that you can employ is when a user is clearly using your product a lot. That might show up in the metrics as:

- Logging in multiple times over a period of time
- Spending multiple hours with the product
- Using all of the features available multiple times
- Installing add-ons that you might have made available

In this case, your product could message the user to let them know that there are even more powerful features available in the paid version of the product.

## Advanced Features

TurboTax (https://turbotax.intuit.com/) is a great case study on freemium conversion, as they've employed and experimented with a number of techniques. Tax forms that can be filed via the 1040EZ used to be free to all users. This is generally a simpler form targeting individuals with a less complicated financial position. These individuals are also less likely to pay for tax services, so they likely aren't "losing out" on much return. Now once those users buy a house and want to file a mortgage tax deduction, they will be forced to itemize and graduate to the 1040 form and hence convert or pay. This strategy is all about giving away lower valued, more commoditized features and monetizing more advanced capabilities.

## Product Results

One of the most powerful ways to encourage free trial users to convert is by tracking and showing the results they're getting from using your product. If your product is an e-commerce platform that helps sell widgets, for example, and you see that the user sold a widget using your software, this can be an apt time to reinforce the benefits of your product while also encouraging them to upgrade to the full version. Maybe they get an in-app reminder about how the full version of the software offers even more features that makes it even easier to sell widgets.

## SUMMARY

While a sales team remains essential for turning leads into customers, product-led companies recognize the power of the product in driving conversions too. You can turn your product into a sales engine by measuring user behavior and developing automated triggers that encourage users to commit to becoming customers. But, once you've converted a customer—or even just brought in a new user from an existing customer—it becomes essential to get them up and running inside the product as quickly as possible with a goal of maximizing their experience. That topic, onboarding, is where we turn next.

# CHAPTER 7

# Getting Customers Off to a Fast Start Through Onboarding

I t takes a tenth of a second to form a first impression of another person. Maybe we notice their body language, how they're dressed, or a small and subtle gesture of kindness or consideration. These are indelible moments in the formation of any relationship. This is particularly important given the competition for our attention today. That first impression prompts us to make a fateful decision: Is this more interesting than the next thing?

The same is true in software products. The first impression tells you whether this is a product worth your scarce time and attention. Users love it, or they leave it. These first impressions welcome users in, or drive them away.

Getting the first impression right begins with an understanding of what your users are seeking to accomplish. Think of the last time you contacted a large institution—say, a phone company or an insurance provider. If you used a telephone, you almost certainly dealt with an interactive voice response (IVR) system that offered a menu of options delivered in a painfully monotone, torturously-slow cadence that probably felt more like a directory of their departments than a useful mechanism for your own problem solving. Once you've connected with a live human, chances are that they asked you to repeat information they should already know (either because you just provided it—or because, well, you're their customer). It's hard to imagine this sort of self-involvement and tone deafness working in any other type of relationship in life.

Yet, somehow, that's what we expect. These experiences leave the impression that your time isn't valued, that the company is imposing its own internal madness, not seeking to understand and resolve your particular need. Who exactly is the customer in this scenario, you might ask?

This is an example of *inside-out* thinking, which is the tendency to design an experience from the perspective of your company's goals and constraints instead of the needs and desires of your customer. The opposite, of course, is the better starting point: designing the experience from the *outside-in*, through the lens of where the user is in their journey, who they are and what they need, and what they're trying to achieve inside your product.

There's a temptation in designing a customer experience to focus on your company's needs first. Nobody does this intentionally. In fact, I've never encountered a company that doesn't, on some level, place its customer at the center of their mission. But it's so easy to lose the thread on this mission when it comes time to prioritize resources and investments.

Many companies end up focusing on their own goals first because, well, these are what they know best—and understanding what the user is trying to accomplish requires substantial effort. Or, if they design the experience from the perspective of the user, they do so superficially, neglecting the fine details that make the experience easy and delightful. Why? Because these insights are rarely apparent on the surface. It takes more time and effort to get to them.

To deliver a great first experience, many companies use humans to introduce and onboard new customers and users. Product-led businesses need to shift their thinking from how humans can create the best first-use experience to how the product itself can. Even when you try and set up an onboarding call with a new B2B customer, for example, not everyone might show up. That means you need ways for the product itself to do more of the heavy lifting and drive the onboarding process on its own.

Onboarding is a critical part of the customer experience because it's not necessarily a linear process. Onboarding influences the trial experience (if there is one), which affects conversion (people buying). If there's no trial, it influences customer health (and ultimately the renewal). Depending on your desired customer experience, onboarding affects different measures and outcomes, but it's critically important.

## CRITICAL EVENTS AND AHA MOMENTS

In Chapter 1, "Start with the End in Mind," we talked about identifying the critical events in your product that correlate with the key performance indicators that drive your business. For example, if you offer a trial or freemium product, one of your key performance indicators is probably the conversion rate of free to paid users. You probably have additional KPIs associated with account health and growth over time. But because KPIs measuring conversion, retention, and expansion are lagging indicators, you need to pair them with leading indicators that predict these outcomes.

This is where onboarding enters the picture. In the onboarding phase, you are seeking to make the right first impression and to create habits that stick in order to keep users coming back. But you're also trying to drive users to perform the key actions that are the leading indicators of the business outcomes you desire.

Back to our Citrix example we shared in the prior chapter: They are primarily an inbound business, which means that new customers are acquired in large part through trial conversions. As a highly product-led organization, the team identified the three key actions in their product that correlated to high conversion rates as follows:

1. Adding a new user
2. Uploading a document
3. Returning to the product within 10 days

With this knowledge, guess which behaviors they reinforced when onboarding new trial users? You guessed it: these three actions. Driving users to complete these actions lifted free-to-paid conversion rates by 11 percent.

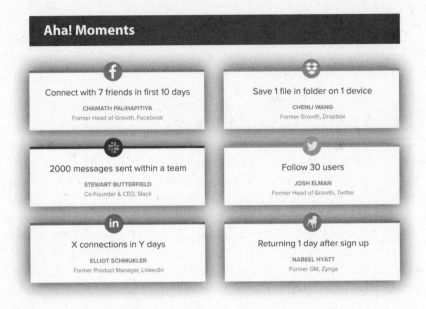

**FIGURE 7.1**   Famous Aha Moments
*Source:* Pendo

You may also think of these as "aha moments," which are when users recognize the distinct value of your product and become committed for the long haul. For example, as featured in Figure 7.1, Facebook knows that when a user connects with seven friends in the first 10 days, they have a much higher likelihood of becoming a regular user. Likewise, Slack knows that 2,000 messages sent within a team is the magic number of exchanges for building a habit that sticks.

Identifying these critical events and aha moments in your business requires the application of data science, using techniques like multivariate regression analysis to uncover statistically significant correlations of certain variables (in this case, user behaviors and actions) with specific desired outcomes (in this case, conversion, retention, and growth). Once you've identified these leading indicators, you can design an onboarding experience that drives new users to engage with your product in a way that stacks the odds in your favor.

## CREATING HABITS THAT STICK

The ultimate goal in designing a first-use experience is to encourage users to develop habits that stick. There's a wide range of research and business writing on the field of behavioral economics targeted at business strategy, marketing, and product and user experience design that looks to the role of feedback and reward systems as the underpinnings to human motivation. In his seminal book on the topic, *Hooked* (Portfolio, 2014), Nir Eyal proposes a model for product design that brings to mind something out of a Las Vegas casino:

- A trigger brings a user into the product for the first time—say, an alluring theme or tone to draw their attention to a video-poker game
- The user is asked to perform an action—for instance, play a first hand of cards for free
- Which yields a reward for the user—for example, some bonus money for trying the game
- Which compels the user to make an investment back into the product—for instance, by investing their bonus money in another hand
- Which, in combination, compels them to use the product over and over again, playing multiple hands

It's a virtuous—or virulent—cycle. It's no great surprise that Vegas casinos are so large and lavish with all of their gilded adornments. This stuff works. The human brain is a reward-seeking machine. But Eyal is careful to point out the ethics of intentionally designing habit-forming products. It can be a slippery slope. Today, social media addiction is said to contribute to depression, anxiety, and even suicide in teens and young adults. Using behavioral economics to shape the first-use experiences in your product can be good for business, to be sure. But it should be done with a first-principle golden rule ethic of helping, not harming, users. A good rule of thumb is to ask one simple question: Are we leading users to something valuable that will make their life better, or are we playing games with their emotions for our own gains? Using a reward system inside your product is perfectly reasonable for the former, but it has the potential to backfire when associated with the latter. Of course, humans are also wired to rationalize behavior. Try to answer this question honestly.

## DESIGNING ONBOARDING EXPERIENCES

Think of the last time that you visited an upscale restaurant or fine hotel. Even if you didn't stay there, recall a time you stepped inside the Four Seasons, the Ritz Carlton, or some small boutique hotel or B&B you visited on vacation. How did you feel when you walked into the lobby for the first time? You were probably impressed by the attention to detail—the thoughtful touches. If you were staying there, someone greeted you and offered to take your bags. Then they probably pointed you—or maybe even escorted you—to the registration desk. The registration clerk smiled and asked a few questions to get you checked in, and then pointed out some of the various amenities of the hotel before showing you to the elevators. Pretty simple, right? And it also felt good. They made you feel welcomed and appreciated.

That's the sort of experience you want to design inside your products. Of course, users often feel just the opposite, where their first-use experience becomes more like a blank stare than a concierge experience. New users shouldn't feel like strangers in a strange land, but like welcomed participants in an exciting new place. Getting this experience right requires attention to detail.

While the customer journey starts long before a company buys your product, the product journey begins with onboarding. Get it wrong, and churn becomes easy to predict. But get it right, and expansion becomes inevitable: One feature leads to the next, adoption maps to value, and new use cases emerge, opening doors to new verticals and new personas.

There's also a couple of aspects of onboarding that tend to get overlooked. For one, onboarding looks different for B2C and B2B companies. In the B2C world, it's all about making first impressions for individual consumers. But in the B2B world, onboarding must factor organizational or administrative issues. Think about it: You've signed up a group of users from an organization, some of whom might not even use or administer the product. They might just be the ones who purchased it. You need to account for these variables by personalizing the onboarding experience based on the role of those users.

The other key piece of this equation is that people inside an organization change over time. They might change roles and not need to use the product anymore, or they might even leave the organization altogether. After all, I've been told that the average tenure of an employee these days is just 18 months. That opens the door for new users of the product who now need to be onboarded. What this means is that onboarding isn't just a one-and-done activity; it's something you might do over and over, potentially for years. And if you overlook the commitment this requires, you risk confusing users, and ultimately, losing that customer.

So how do you deliver a complete onboarding experience? Start with a core product-led notion: Guide the user toward behaviors correlated with success. This requires both an ability to identify your most successful users and data to pattern-match their behaviors with results.

In other words, a product-led onboarding process is rooted in product analytics. Lessons from past users can help new customers enjoy the shortest path to value. Continually analyze this process to refine and improve it along the way, and focus heavily on guiding users early and often toward a cumulative experience that defines the product journey. As you gather more data, customize and iterate the onboarding process to drive each user along a journey most relevant to them.

Many product teams are actively re-evaluating their approach to user onboarding. Rather than treating it as a distinct process outside of the product, they are working to make onboarding content and flows a core component of the product experience. With this approach, when a new user logs into the product or new features are released, relevant training content is pushed directly to the user.

In-app training content can take the form of announcements, embedded video tutorials, links to Knowledge Base articles, or other help content, and step-by-step walk-throughs that take users through specific tasks in the product. Education in-app becomes much more contextual to the user and is more likely to be consumed. However, product teams need to be sure that the content they push into the product is relevant and not unnecessarily cluttering the user experience.

## PERSONALIZING THE ONBOARDING EXPERIENCE

Most organizations have sufficient information and context about their users to tailor the onboarding experience in a way that makes the content as relevant as possible to the user. Basic elements of the user profile such as role, plan level, or customer size can help to determine whether education content will be helpful to a specific user. User behavior and demonstrated proficiency can determine how much training they need when new features are shipped.

New tools make it easier for product teams to leverage this data as a part of their onboarding development. These tools pull user context through integrations with key customer systems such as CRM and marketing automation. They use product usage data to target content based on user behavior. With point-and-click authoring, they allow product, UX, and customer education managers to create and push personalized training content into the product experience without having to rely on engineering resources.

Consider an example of this practice in action. CareCloud (https://www.carecloud.com/) is a SaaS company that provides electronic health record and billing tools for medical practices. They've invested a lot in designing really simple and thoughtful onboarding experiences that delight new users, knowing that these users—often administrative staff in doctor's offices—aren't always heavy users of business software. They want to make the experience for their new users something that's welcoming, not intimidating.

Adam Siegel[1], an education content specialist at the company describes this onboarding as much about art as it is about science,

---

[1] Adam Siegel, "Proactive Onboarding: Driving Success w/ KPIs and Accountability", presentation given during Pendomonium 2019

pointing out that the content should be delivered in an easily consumable format and only when it's meaningful to the user. This means throwing away tedious manuals and long lists of instructions and delivering bite-sized guidance, just in time, when it's needed by users, directly inside the product itself.

The hard truth, as the CareCloud team points out, is that users don't have the time and attention to learn everything that you might want to throw their way. He describes the users' motivation, cleverly, like a health bar in a video game, as seen in Figure 7.2:

**FIGURE 7.2**   Full health bar
*Source:* Pendo

**FIGURE 7.3**   Mid health bar
*Source:* Pendo

**FIGURE 7.4**   Low health bar
*Source:* Pendo

Every time users go to a screen that doesn't add value, or they click another button, they lose motivation. It's a race against the clock.

Where your goal is to get users to value before the health bar runs out!

It's a great way to think about how to design user onboarding. It requires a very intentional approach to delivering just what users need, when they need it, and doing so in an inviting, motivating, and fundamentally human way. That's why onboarding really is an art.

The following are some onboarding tips from the CareCloud team:

**Get users to engage with the features that they want and need**: Your product analytics, user feedback, and, frankly, general knowledge should tell you which features, and combination of features, are most valuable to which roles. Segment users and target onboarding flows based on the features that will be most relevant and powerful to them.

**Acknowledge users' accomplishments**: Give users some feedback. Let them know that they're making progress. Celebrate it. Believe it or not, this sort of dialogue has the effect of cheering them on from the sidelines and motivating them to take the next step.

**Gamify the experience**: As we learned from Nir Eyal, humans are reward-seeking machines. They're wired to want to win, even when the games are low stakes. Find ways to show users the progress they're making and how they stack up.

Let's take a look at how this shows up in their first-use experience.

CareCloud begins with a framework, represented by Figure 7.5, which illustrates the user journey, from first use to return visit and continued usage over time. They've reduced this to four phases as illustrated in the lifecycle below,

1. **Onboarding**: This refers to the first-use experience for new users, ensuring that they're oriented to the product and guided to discover value based on their specific role and jobs to be done. Using analytics, they track the completion of onboarding steps so that they can intervene where users lose track or fall off.
2. **Training**: This is where CareCloud drives onboarded users to the sort of proficiency that will help them make the product a

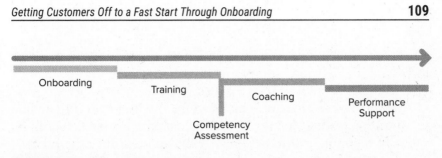

**FIGURE 7.5**   Onboarding Journey
*Source:* Pendo

daily habit. This means identifying and correcting incomplete steps in their onboarding experience. They support users with training in multiple modalities, including a Knowledge Base for capturing, indexing, and organizing the answers to frequently asked questions and enabling users to self-serve as they run into issues. It also includes in-app dialogues with users that are designed to anticipate and fulfill their needs based on their user persona and their observed behavior inside the product. In many cases, these in-app guides utilize the same content stored within the knowledge base and simply serve it up in context, just in time.

3. **Coaching**: This is where humans get involved to help remediate issues detected in the onboarding experience as a way to intervene ahead of potential downstream issues. By utilizing analytics that measure the onboarding experience, these coaches can tailor and target their reinforcement to the areas that need conspicuous attention.

4. **Performance support**: This where all of these capabilities—analytics, in-app training, and people-based coaching—are utilized over the full breadth of the product journey and customer lifecycle. Onboarding, it's important to note, should never be viewed as one-and-done; it's an ongoing process of user support from the first use experience to the end of the commercial relationship. Ensuring that your product delivers value to users means unending vigilance and diligence in guiding users over time.

The CareCloud first-use experience encompasses three key steps:

**Step 1: The Welcome** The Welcome is where users are invited into the product for the first time, using a personalized email with a simple call to action that draws them into the product (see Figure 7.6).

**Step 2: Learning the Basics** As shown in Figure 7.7, this is where users are guided to set up their account and given a small pat on the back for their effort. (It seems silly, but the accumulation of these small rewards, however low-stakes they may be, have an impact on the reward-seeking human.) They then invite the new user into the onboarding sequence to give them a guided tour of the product. Because CareCloud knows a bit about the user, this walk-through is targeted to their persona.

**Step 3: Building the Foundations** Once the new user has been given an orientation, they're invited to choose their own

**FIGURE 7.6** Onboarding Email
*Source:* CareCloud and Pendo

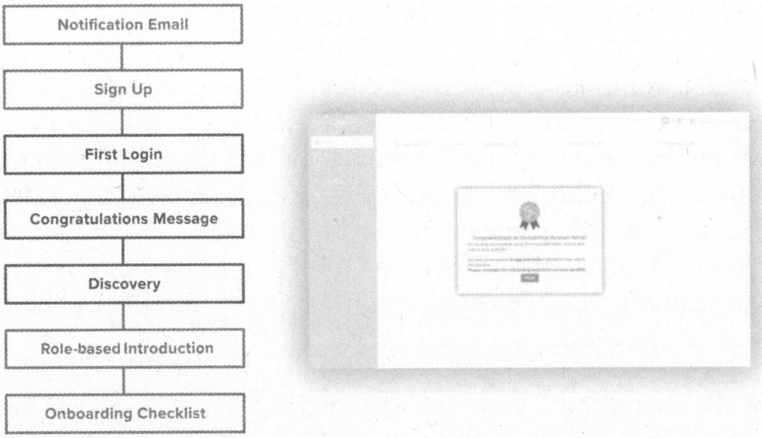

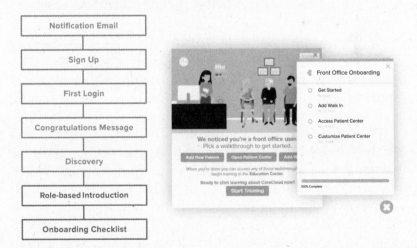

**FIGURE 7.7**   Welcoming Users
*Source:* Pendo and CareCloud

adventure to drill down into the areas that are most relevant and useful for their persona, as shown in Figure 7.8. This training is designed to build the foundations in sequence with a well-defined set of onboarding steps that CareCloud wants users to complete for basic proficiency.

**FIGURE 7.8**   Customer Training
*Source:* Pendo and CareCloud

## THE BUILDING BLOCKS OF USER ONBOARDING

There are multiple engagement modalities to consider when designing an onboarding experience. A well-designed experience never uses just one modality, but threads them thoughtfully across multiple touchpoints and interactions. Think of it as the palette from which an artist may draw in the creation of some sort of mixed-media installation. The end product is the combination of many different things, thoughtfully applied. Your palette should include the following:

**Walk-throughs** These are guided in-app dialogues that "walk" the user through the key features that they can utilize and introduce the sequence of steps required to complete a task or workflow. The key is to design these walk-throughs with three goals in mind:

1. To sell the value of the features, persuading users that they're worthy of their attention
2. To link features together, so that users can envision how to use them to complete a task
3. To help users to "learn by doing," inviting them to take actions along the way

Walk-throughs are most useful in support of first-use experiences, either for onboarding a brand-new user with limited familiarity with your product or guiding an existing user through the steps necessary to take advantage of a new feature or an existing feature they haven't utilized.

Walk-throughs can be triggered by user behavior and can be targeted to particular user segments, accounts, or individual visitors. While helpful to relay more complicated information or multi-step processes, walk-throughs can quickly become overwhelming for users if they are used too generously. Be sure to measure completion and drop-off rates to identify if the walk-through is too long, or if any steps are too complicated.

**Tooltips** These are in-app tutorials that are made available to users when they hover over key features. These are the most pervasively available and least interruptive form of user engagement because they are only visible when a user elects to view them. Tooltips are particularly useful for explaining features that are perhaps less comprehensible by name alone.

The most common type of tooltips are "hovers," which are messages that appear when the user moves their cursor over a navigation menu, interactive element, or predetermined "hotspot." Tooltips should primarily be used to provide supplemental explanations for features that would otherwise clutter the UI if permanently displayed.

**Lightboxes** Also called a "pop-up" or a "modal," lightboxes are a style of in-app message that often dims or darkens the rest of the page to emphasize the content. They are interstitial messages that are meant to draw attention to a specific announcement or call to action when a user logs in or at some other point on the product journey. For example, lightboxes may be used to announce scheduled downtime, drive registration to a webinar, or to let a user know that payment is overdue on their account. Some lightboxes even prevent the user from interacting with the rest of the page until the message is dismissed.

Lightboxes have the potential to be the most intrusive form of engagement, particularly when they're not designed thoughtfully and targeted with precision.

**Landing pad/placemat** This is a type of lightbox or full-screen takeover that provides the end user with options on where to explore. They create a bit of a sense of choose-your-own-adventure for users to prompt them on where they can go next inside your app.

**Blank slates** These are the "empty" state for parts of your user interface. Instead of welcoming your users with an intimidating blank page, this is an opportunity to educate the user on what to do next or what might be possible for them to create inside the product. Some products avoid these states by loading sample or demo data into trial or new user experiences. While this may help, it could be confusing for the end user as it may not reflect their specific use case.

**Knowledge base** This is a repository of everything a user may ever want to know about your product, including answers to frequently—and not so frequently—asked questions. Notably, the knowledge base indexes and organizes this information and makes it discoverable by users on a self-service basis or rendered as a content object within a tooltip, walk-through, or lightbox.

**Email** We're all only too familiar with email, but it is an important way to engage users, at first use (before they're a user of the product) and when usage lapses. While engagement via email isn't always the greatest, it's an important communication vehicle to augment in-app engagement.

**Don't forget people!** Ultimately, a product-led experience isn't meant to replace people altogether but to scale their knowledge to support the user better on their product journey. And there are important moments along that journey when there is absolutely no substitute for one-on-one human interaction. Examples might include the need to remediate an issue, resolve a frustration, understand a need, or simply ensure that the user feels heard and appreciated. The key is knowing where and when to apply that human intervention by using data to measure engagement over time and never to rely on this human intervention as the primary mode of interaction with users. That, of course, will never scale.

## A WORD ON TIMING AND TARGETING

It's important to remember that getting targeting right will always make the difference between engagement that's welcomed by users and engagement that's seen as annoying, intrusive, or worse. Think back to the example of the hotel concierge. Now compare that generally helpful experience to a carnival barker trying to get your attention as you walk along an arcade. In both cases, they have commercial agendas, but the concierge is focused on earning your business by anticipating and fulfilling your needs—not beating you over the head with the equivalent of a blunt instrument to shake a few nickels from your pockets. To your users, engagement that isn't thoughtfully timed and targeted will feel more like a carnival barker than a concierge.

It's also important to get the timing right. Few people have the time these days to sit down and read through a manual. That's why onboarding should be served up in spoon-fed bites, progressively over time.

## PROGRESSIVE DISCLOSURE

According to Jacob Nielsen, a consultant and author who is arguably the most notable and celebrated expert in user experience design, progressive disclosure *"defers advanced or rarely used features to a secondary screen, making applications easier to learn and less error-prone."*[2]

Nielsen suggests holding back features that, despite your understandable pride and barely contained excitement to share with your users, may only serve to confuse and distract as they're learning how to use your product.

Consider the example of Choozle (https://choozle.com/), a digital advertising platform that offers a multitude of options for its users to create customized campaigns. The catch is that it might have too many features, which can be overwhelming for some users. Occasionally, a customer would even churn on the assumption that a feature they really needed wasn't offered—even though it was there all along. To boost awareness of these features, Choozle built out a communications strategy with Pendo's in-app messaging and guidance capabilities at its core. Each month, Choozle built a campaign around a single feature, with a series of Pendo guides delivered at multiple points within the platform, including on the

---

[2]Nielsen Norman Group, "Progressive Disclosure": https://www.nngroup.com/articles/progressive-disclosure/

homepage as a user logs in and on the campaign setup page, where features live. For example, one campaign promoted cross-device targeting, which extended the reach of an advertising campaign by delivering ads to the same person across all of their devices. Since it was activated by a small toggle switch in the campaign setup interface, it was often overlooked. By adopting this progressive disclosure strategy, Choozle saw a massive 154 percent increase in usage of the feature following the month-long campaign, which led to a 205 percent increase in active customers and 40 percent year-over-year revenue growth.

With progressive disclosure, the goal is to make the main thing the main thing, focusing on the most important features first and unveiling additional features in spoon-fed bites over time. It's important to note that exactly what the main thing is often varies by persona or individual based on their jobs to be done and observed behaviors inside the product. With onboarding, it's important to avoid the one-size-fits-all trap at the risk of all sizes fitting none.

## GETTING THE ONBOARDING EXPERIENCE RIGHT

First impressions count for a lot. Getting them right requires empathy with your users, an inclination to sweat the details, and a willingness to exercise restraint based on the premise that, in the business of user onboarding, timing is everything, and less is often more.

The CareCloud team offers some great summary advice for designing onboarding:

1. **Focus on the user, not the product**: While it's often tempting to show off everything your product has to offer, this would be missing the point. Users don't really care about your product. They care about whatever job they're looking to accomplish. Focus on that.
2. **Fast track users to value**: Make the main thing the main thing, guiding users to the features and use cases that will maximize the early inkling of value so they come back for more.

3. **Segment by persona**: Recognize that the needs and expectations of users vary by persona, and be sure to design onboarding experiences with multiple personas in mind and segment and target these experiences accordingly.

4. **Never show an empty progress bar**: You're in a bit of a race against time to demonstrate value. Never take that for granted. Show your users that you're working on their behalf and not simply wasting their time. Keep them engaged with the small rewards of feedback and acknowledgment to be sure that they continue along for the ride.

## EVOLVING THROUGH EXPERIMENTATION

How do you know what effective onboarding looks like? You know it when you see it because it helps you achieve certain outcomes for your business and your users. But how do you know in advance what onboarding experiences will drive these outcomes? The simple answer is: You run experiments.

French physiologist Claude Bernard is noted as one of the pioneers of experiment-driven learning, popularizing a method of blind experimentation to ensure objectivity in scientific methods. Bernard said that observation is a passive science. Experimentation is an active science. Observation is what leads you to a hypothesis, but experimentation is how you test it.

In the same way that a digital marketer tests a variety of subject lines in emails, or copy and images in advertising, you'll want to do the same with your onboarding experiences. The outside-in research and reflection that you've done helps you form hypotheses. However, running experiments is how you know for sure which messages, sequences, and channels are best for helping new users through the crucial steps of learning how to use your product.

In short, increased engagement with onboarding content leads to more proficient users who realize product value at a much quicker pace. By leveraging data to power an in-app onboarding and user training experience, product teams can increase customer retention rates and reduce reliance on customer success and support interventions to make users successful in the product.

## ONBOARDING NEVER ENDS

When is onboarding complete? It's a deceptively tricky question to answer. Why? Because the training required for a new user varies by individual based on their skill set, their technical aptitude, and their general tolerance for things unfamiliar and new. One person's easy is another person's complex. One person will get it immediately, while another will take a while. RE/MAX offers a great example of this. When training real estate agents on their various software applications, they use insights from how agents are progressing through an automated onboarding process to determine where they might need to supplement with live training.

That's not to say you can't—or shouldn't—answer the question of when onboarding ends. (You can and you should!) It's just that how you measure completion rates will follow the law of averages. Segmentation, of course, brings you closer to the truth by allowing you to measure completion rates by user segment or cohort. At the most basic level, you'll want to measure completion of the path to proficiency I described above. Ensuring that everyone has completed these basic steps will provide the foundation upon which you can build more advanced competency inside your product.

Next, you'll want to measure completion of key actions inside your product that act as leading indicators for the business outcomes you're looking to achieve. Designing your onboarding experience with these initial experiences in mind earns you the right to train users on more advanced capabilities that will ultimately drive more engagement and value over time.

Think of this as the somewhat nebulous distinction between onboarding and adoption. Too often, the onboarding phase ends once these basic boxes are checked. The reality is, to achieve lasting loyalty to your software applications, onboarding never ends. It's built around the principles of progressive disclosure, which intelligently reveals new learning content to users as they indicate need and readiness. It also accounts for the fact that your product is not a static artifact—it's a living organism. As you roll out new features and make changes in your UI, you start the cycle of onboarding all over again.

The key is user data. You can't deliver a good onboarding experience for new users if you don't know where they've been and where they're trying to go. This is particularly true for the process of training existing users. It's not unlike contacting customer support at your bank and having to catch them up on everything they ought to know about you. That's incredibly annoying. By the same principle, training your users should begin where they left off. That requires measurement of their behavior and onboarding experiences that match where they are in the product journey.

## SUMMARY

In this chapter, we discussed ways that you can engage your customers immediately with your product, as well as some ways to personalize their onboarding experience to help ensure that they get off to the best possible start with your product. We'll build on these lessons in the next chapter, as we dig into how you can identify and remove obstacles that might prevent your customers from engaging more deeply with your product. These strategies ensure your customers feel your product is providing them real value.

# CHAPTER 8

# Delivering Value

**M**uch of our focus in this book has been on the ways that we can improve the success of our products. However, from a product design perspective, it's also incredibly valuable to understand how your customers define success. To understand why your customer is buying your product, you need to track how you are solving their pain. You need to understand how they measure success and then give them those measures. If you can share how you are measuring the value you are generating for them—their return on investment (ROI), for example—you can win a customer for life. And ultimately, it's your job to measure and improve your customer's ability to realize that value efficiently. Consider the case of Corey Thomas, the CEO and founder of Rapid7, a provider of cybersecurity services, who has prioritized creating a customer-centric organization from the start. He's found that to be extremely valuable in a market like cybersecurity, where customers under extreme stress and pressure are looking for help. "If we can retain customers well, those customers will buy more and build more and do more for the brand and become advocates for the brand over time," Thomas said in an interview with Ken Freeman, a professor at Boston University's Questrom School of Business. "It makes good economic sense."[1]

In this chapter, we'll share the importance of measuring the customer journey and how to optimize it for realizing value.

## UNDERSTANDING THE CUSTOMER JOURNEY

In a previous chapter, we discussed journey maps as a mechanism for understanding the customer's needs and they change at different

---

[1] "Conversations with Ken: Corey Thomas," *YouTube*, October 26, 2017; https://www.youtube.com/watch?v=V52wrz4OJwI

stages of their interaction with your company. This is a useful lens for understanding the specific tasks that users have in mind when they log in to your product. Understanding these journeys requires a fair amount of interaction with customers, but you can also learn a lot by simply observing and learning from user behavior inside your application.

Why close observation is so important is best illustrated by a famous meme in user experience circles that highlights the difference between the designed path and the desired path. In the best of circumstances, these two paths intersect. Of course, in reality, they often don't, as exemplified by the photo in Figure 8.1.

Here, the task the person in this picture is trying to complete is pretty obvious: to walk from one side of a park to the other. How they prefer to complete that task is much less obvious—or it *was*

**FIGURE 8.1**   The Difference Between the Designed Path and the Desired Path
*Source:* Pendo

much less obvious to the landscape architects responsible for this failed design. The lesson? Begin with a hypothesis, but don't pour the concrete until it's been sufficiently tested in the wild.

How you test these hypotheses begins with data—specifically the sort of data that reveal the sequence of steps taken by users inside your product. By exploring the paths taken by users, as exemplified in Figure 8.2, you can start to think about the experience you create and the behaviors you shape from the perspective of the tasks that users want to perform, and, crucially, how they want to perform them.

In Figure 8.2, you see the sequential actions taken by users inside an application. You can see where they spend time by key features and, more importantly for this purpose, the order in which they use those features. Once you've explored this data, patterns start to emerge—patterns you can use to design the right experiences inside your product.

Start by asking yourself questions like: Why do users come to my product? What's the first thing they do when they get there? What's the thing they do most frequently (if they had to do one)?

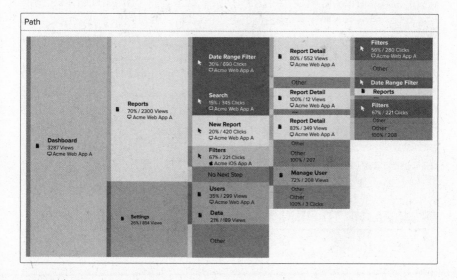

**FIGURE 8.2** Exploring User Paths Inside an Application
*Source:* Pendo

The answers to these questions deliver great insight. Given that we are all competing for attention, attracting a user to our product is a success. Whatever they did was likely the root cause and possibly the highest valued capability. In Chapter 2, we introduced the Superhuman survey to ask customers what they don't want to lose, but we can also observe this behavior in the data.

How do users get to these core capabilities? How efficient is this journey? Are there blockages or challenges with completing the function? All of these answers have an effect on the overall customer experience. Generally, you want to reduce friction for your users to accomplish the key areas of the product.

One Pendo customer, Invoca (https://www.invoca.com/), offers a product called Call Intelligence, which is a platform for marketers to get real-time campaign data to understand better why customers are calling, who's calling, and what's being said in conversations. But when the Invoca team launched a new user interface, they noticed something strange: Some users had found a way to bypass the new UI and were going directly to some of the older pages.

By using Pendo, the Invoca team learned which specific users were using the old features, and they reached out to them to find out why they were bypassing the new UI. What they learned was that their users were looking to access a certain dashboard that was now buried under a "Reports" option, which added several clicks for users to access. Armed with this new information, Invoca was able to make this data more easily accessible in the updated UI. They deployed several guides reminding users to change their browser bookmarks (the primary source of traffic to the old page). Several weeks after deploying the guides, visits to the old page dried up completely.

## FROM PATHS TO FUNNELS

Once you understand the tasks that users are trying to complete and the paths they prefer, you can measure these explicit steps as a progressive funnel, such as the one seen in Figure 8.3. In the same way that a digital marketer measures and optimizes the purchase

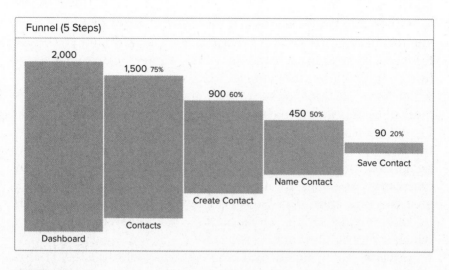

**FIGURE 8.3** Creating Funnels Inside an Application
*Source:* Pendo

path on a commerce site, these funnels help you understand how users convert from one step to another as they complete tasks within your product and fine-tune the experience where conversion between steps isn't up to snuff.

## IDENTIFYING BLOCKAGES AND FRUSTRATION

Optimizing task completion requires the continuous discipline of close observation and frequent minor adjustments to the user experience, both through changes to UX layout and functionality itself, as well as streamlining more difficult parts of the user experience with in-app tooltips, guides, and tutorials. Targeting these optimizations requires observation at a variety of altitudes. Higher-level altitudes include using techniques like paths and funnels to understand how users journey across applications. It also involves assessing overall customer sentiment using surveys like NPS or CSAT, which we discussed in Chapters 2 and 4. On a lower-level altitude, we can look at data like completion percentages on forms or specific feedback on a feature that just shipped.

Once you identify potential drop-offs in task completion, it begs an obvious question: Why? The answer is informed by direct feedback from users, but you may also want to watch your users in action, up close and personal. That's the role of session replay, which you can think of as something like the practice tapes that football teams watch together before game day. It's a way to see exactly what went right and what went wrong in order to adjust future performance. By reviewing the sessions, product teams can better understand what it feels like for the user. The combination of journey analytics for understanding paths and funnels is a great starting point because it can highlight where to drill down by looking at specific sessions themselves through session replay, which we introduced in Chapter 3.

Session replay vendor FullStory (https://www.fullstory.com/), whom we mentioned earlier in the book, has popularized the idea of "rage clicks" as an observable proxy for friction in the user experience and the attendant frustration it creates for users. *Rage Clicks* are the virtual equivalent of mashing an unresponsive button on a vending machine—only it's a mouse button. Rage clicks are a digital signal of a user's deep annoyance with your site's UX.

No product team ever sets out to build software with anything but an idea of a job to be done. But the specific jobs that customers have in mind—and their desired paths they want to follow in completing them—aren't always the ones that you originally envisioned. As these two perspectives diverge, your product becomes progressively less useful. As a product leader, the onus is on you to keep these things in close alignment. The products that get this alignment right have the best odds of forming enduring habits with their users.

Consider when LabCorp (https://www.labcorp.com/), the global life sciences company, learned that many of its patients were dropping out of the registration process to use the LabCorp Patient mobile app. By studying users' journeys, they found that their system would return an error message if the user added an extra space after their name. Once they understood the scope of this issue, they could prioritize the fix with their counterparts in engineering. The registration experience improved dramatically without users ever knowing, and the percentage of dropouts dropped markedly. Analyzing customer path data led to another surprising discovery: Some users weren't completing their registration because a third-party authentication tool was taking so long to load that patients were often abandoning the process. LabCorp wouldn't have been able to uncover these subtle issues without truly understanding the paths that different cohorts of users were following. Within weeks of identifying and fixing just these two issues, support tickets plummeted. Friction-related tickets dropped from several thousand to about a hundred over the course of several months, cutting their backlog by 99 percent.

Another example comes from Stacy Brown-Philpot, the CEO of TaskRabbit, a key supplier of work in the gig economy. At its start, the company posted available jobs via its website. But, given that many gig workers would move from task to task throughout the day, it wasn't always realistic for them to access a computer or laptop to find their next gig. At the same time, someone who might need help with a task might also be far from a computer when they need it. TaskRabbit finally eliminated that point of constraint by investing heavily in their mobile product—which helped double the size of their business. "We're now half mobile, more than double than before," Brown-Philpot said in a 2017 interview with the Stanford Graduate School of Business. "We took the experience and learned what the customer really wants and invested in the technology that really works for her. You can post a task in three clicks."[2]

## IDENTIFYING FRICTION: PINPOINT DROP-OFFS AND BOTTLENECKS

A primary goal in designing more intuitive experiences for users is to remove friction so that new users can find their way to the features and capabilities that keep them coming back over and over

---

[2] Mary Duan, "Stacy Brown-Philpot: Hire Leaders, Leave to Take Risks," *Insights by Stanford Business*, April 18, 2017; https://www.gsb.stanford.edu/insights/stacy-brown-philpot-hire-leaders-leave-take-risks

again. Friction can be thought of as any extra steps, or "clicky" and unintuitive parts of the experience, which add what social scientists call "cognitive load." Think of *cognitive load* as activities assigned to a user's working memory that distract from another competing activity. Even small amounts of friction can add cognitive load, which will drive users away from your product.

One of the most common and obvious points of friction is the email validation step sitting between the completion of a form and authentication in the product. This is often present in a self-service trial or freemium mode, where you're seeking to convert an anonymous visitor on your website into a known user inside your product.

The step serves a perfectly useful purpose in ensuring the quality and integrity of contact information; a fake email address makes it much harder to engage a user who has disengaged from your product. But adding this step can reduce conversion rates by as much as 50 percent. Why? Because it requires context switching—moving from one screen or application to another—which adds cognitive load for the user. Who knows what delightfully shiny objects may intervene to capture their attention in these sacred moments?

Friction will always be present in any user experience. The point isn't to eliminate it entirely, but to understand which friction points lead to drop-offs on the conversion path or in usage over time, and to stomp those out like the nasty bugs they most certainly are. Then, design the experience and layer on contextual guidance to help users find their way.

## REMOVING FRICTION

Friction can take many different forms when it comes to hindering how a customer might interact with a product. In a B2C application, for example, friction points will likely be very product focused, such as a bug with using a particular feature. This is where you can use leading indicators like health scores (a topic we will explore in more detail later in Chapter 10, "Renew and Expand: Creating Customers for Life") to understand where your customers might not be leveraging the product as effectively as possible.

The rise of the subscription economy means that it has become easier than ever for customers to switch between vendors or even back out of contracts with few, if any, consequences. This has made customer retention an integral aspect of growth. And because growth begins with products that deliver ongoing value, remaining competitive increasingly depends on the presence of an effective and responsive customer success team. But there's another angle to removing customer friction, especially in the B2B software world—that is, building relationships with customers.

This is why customer success teams represent the eyes, ears, and heart of a product-led organization. They live on the front lines, listening, watching, and helping customers find their way to value. And since a product-led strategy is based on a continuous dialogue with the customer, the success team does not have to depend on instinct and anecdote. They can measure and monitor customer health and happiness using hard data and then communicate customer needs to the entire company.

More than this, a product-led customer success team creates a close partnership between the company and the customer. This involves meeting them at every step of their journey, beginning with their earliest interactions and continuing throughout their relationship. Doing so not only positions them at the front lines for customers, but it also turns them into a pivotal link in the product feedback cycle. They can pair quantifiable usage data with customer feedback and stories, providing crucial context to the improvement process. This helps strengthen the link between customer success, product, and every other team, bringing the entire company into closer alignment.

To get some additional clarity on this issue, I spoke with Mark Freeman, senior director of customer success (CS) at Pendo. Mark has more than a decade of experience in CS at companies like LinkedIn. He has watched the role of CS evolve dramatically over that time. "We used to just focus on lagging indicators like renewal rates or expansion as a measure of customer success," Mark says. "But we're now considering whether we have the right people involved on both our side as well as the customer's." Mark believes this is something that a lot of product-focused companies miss.

"If we don't understand what outcomes our customers want to drive and take ownership of them, while also making sure they feel accountable for those results as well, we'll create friction," he says.

To overcome this potential friction, it's key to have the right people in place to drive accountability to the outcomes the customers want. Mark recalls his goal at a prior software company: to create a great stable of advocates who are part of a network and a community where they can connect and learn from each other. We take a similar approach at Pendo, where one of our values is to have a maniacal focus on customers.

While sometimes that means reacting to problems a customer might be having, Mark and his team are also taking a more proactive approach. My company is really fortunate to have really high customer retention rates, in large part due to the product itself, but also because of the great work that Mark and his team do. But that's not to say that we don't lose customers. One of the primary reasons why customers don't renew their subscriptions with Pendo is because they don't understand whether they are getting a measurable ROI from using the product. Mark's team's role, therefore, is to work with customers to help ensure that they understand the value they get from using the product—to put a plan together that measures if we are delivering on that promise.

"That begins with understanding what outcomes the customer wants from using the product," says Mark. "We might ask a customer, for example, to share the top reason a customer may elect not to renew with Pendo. That way, rather than stretching out our hands and saying, 'How can we help you?', we can flip the model and make suggestions to the customer. We can say something like, 'Based on what you told us, we think we should be doing this' or 'we think you should consider doing this.' It becomes much more of a partnership with the customer where we can be much more effective at removing any friction they might be experiencing."

Mark's job is to take a hands-on, manual approach to reducing friction and improving customer outcomes. But there are a lot of automated and product-led ways to reduce friction too. Many of the onboarding concepts we introduced in Chapter 7 are also built to reduce friction. The same onboarding techniques, where the goal is to have your product educate customers and increase engagement, can be used to optimize any part of the customer journey.

## WHEN YOUR EMPLOYEE IS YOUR USER

Much of our focus in this book has been on how to build products for external customers. But these same lessons apply when your user is someone who works for you—your employee. That's especially true as more and more organizations develop software of their own or look to monitor how their employees are using purchased software to do their jobs. After all, the goal should be to offer your employees tools that they enjoy using and that make them more productive.

Yet, just as importantly, driving a high-quality experience for your employees can be a key factor in how engaged or satisfied they are at work. If the product they use on a daily basis creates friction and makes it harder for them to do their work, they might consider working elsewhere.

For example, I was chatting with the head of a hospital system who mentioned that they had begun tracking the number of clicks their doctors make inside a piece of software they use. What they found was that the doctors who made more clicks were less happy with their jobs. Happier, more satisfied doctors tend to deliver better patient care.

It's also important to think about the software we encounter in our personal lives—social media, games or personal productivity tools. These applications are typically easier and more engaging to use than what we're forced to interact with at work. That dynamic can drive dissatisfaction, low productivity, and, ultimately, employee turnover.

So, when you think about delivering value to your customers throughout your product, don't overlook the opportunities to do the same for your employees.

## SUMMARY

It's critically important to understand what your customers want from your product—and for them to feel like they're receiving significant value from using it. In this chapter, we discussed the customer journey and how, by measuring and then understanding how customers are using your product, you can unlock additional value for them. A key component of that is learning where customers run into "friction" points, or frustrations, and then removing them either automatically through your product or through the help of your customer experience team. But another factor in driving the customer experience in a product-led world is to give customers the opportunity to answer their own questions and solve their own problems while using their product—which is what we'll discuss in the next chapter.

# CHAPTER 9

# Customer Self-Service

A key trend driving software today, especially in a product-led world, is that customers want self-service, digitally-driven experiences. So, while part of serving customers remains a manual process, becoming product led also means automating how and where customers get support, education, and service inside an application. Perhaps more importantly, these capabilities also need to be available in ways that enable the customer to serve themselves. It's how we can make the product experience better for the customer.

## SUPPORT LOAD AND TICKET DEFLECTION

We've all been there. You sit down in front of your computer and log in to a piece of software with a task in mind. Sure, you don't know how to do it, but you figure, "How hard can it be? Software is intuitive, right?"

You poke around for a few minutes, but the capability isn't readily apparent. You focus harder, putting on your "finding eyes"—an expression we use with our kids when they can't find something that's literally right under their nose. Yet after really trying to figure out this software, the functionality continues to elude you—it's not under your nose, or anyone else's.

At this point, you're mildly irritated. You look for that trusty question mark icon or help menu, assuming, generously, that your need is a corner case, thus the advanced feature is less common and therefore less discoverable. The help page, it turns out, isn't all that helpful. It doesn't contain your solution.

Now you're probably ticked. If you're like me, you're muttering profanities. In most cases, you give up. Your task wasn't *that* important, you tell yourself. But what if it was critically important? What if you're trying to register for a class or add a dependent to your health insurance?

So, reluctantly, you reach out to tech support. You fill out a form, which prompts a number of drop-downs (none of which match your particular issue, of course), and you wait for the inhuman auto-responder to tell you your wait time. Hopefully, you'll be free whenever you hear back.

Maybe you get lucky, and the company responds with an answer. Perhaps the answer is even instructive. Depending on the response, you could feel a range of emotions. Validation? "Wow, that was sort of tricky." Irritated? "Why was the solution to a basic problem so painful and convoluted?" Embarrassed? "How am I such an idiot that I missed this?" In any event, you don't feel better about the product you're using.

Why do we have a chapter on support in a product book? No, this isn't some sort of elaborate head fake. Support exists for one reason: because of problems in products. If products were perfect, support likely wouldn't be needed. Some smart-ass will probably cite examples of people misusing desktop computer DVD trays as cupholders to justify the existence of support—making products "idiot-proof" is very difficult. But users are becoming pretty darn savvy, and software is consuming many of the daily life services we take for granted. It won't be long before you'll interface with software to engage with your bank, insurance provider, and healthcare provider. That might already be the case.

Support tickets are excellent measures for product usability. They reflect user confusion and frustration. They contain insights derived from every single engagement. There are several different types of support metrics you might track, each providing a different type of value to product teams.

## Ticket Metrics

Each ticket is instructive about how to improve the product experience. Ticket trends provide high-level views on whether the product requires more or less support. It's important when looking at ticket trends to normalize the data based on your actual user growth. Growth begets more volume, so understanding volume per user provides more insights.

Categorizing tickets is helpful for understanding what part of a product is leading to questions. Basic pie charts highlight which areas of the product provoke the most questions. By trending each area, teams can get a sense of whether they are improving an area of the product or worsening it.

Ticket age is a useful measure for understanding the impact of the problem. Tickets that are open for weeks cause more strain on the customer relationship and are also a source of higher cost to your organization. These issues are also good indicators of areas that could benefit from internal debugging tools. Typically, long-running issues require greater organizational involvement, meaning that you're likely taking your engineering team off of building new features to look at these issues—they are very costly.

## Help Metrics

Remember that fictional story I shared earlier about a user getting frustrated by (a lack of) help within a product? Of course, that presupposed that help was available. That's not always the case today. Try turning off an iPhone X—I need to Google it each and every time. Our smartphones don't come with documentation. In the past, it was common to have office shelves lined with manuals. That doesn't really exist today. Yet, we still recommend that most products come with some documentation—the more expensive the software product, the more likely it requires documentation. But it's important to think of help as support—it's self-service. Any time users ask for support, it's a sign of a product failure, so there is something to learn every time someone clicks the "help" button.

Unlike an iPhone, most web-based products have a Help section. This section is traditionally a repository of documentation explaining how to use the product, with screenshots highlighting common setups. These systems aren't always integrated into the application—in fact, they're more likely to be housed on stand-alone sites. While they typically have valuable content, they require users to search for answers, which is difficult when people have shrinking attention spans and time-sensitive jobs to do.

Product-led companies are changing up the old model. They often embed small help windows directly inside the product's interface. These windows can be contextualized to the user based on who they are and where they are in the product. For example, they might display content for capabilities only available on that page to provide users a quicker solution. This is especially critical for products that offer a variety of capabilities for different sets of users—why make all documentation available to everyone when they only require a slice of it?

These systems aren't just describing product functionality in large blocks of text; they can also walk the user interactively through the product to have them perform the function themselves. This interactive style of support ensures the user learns what to do. It's also measurable. If you notice that users are getting three-quarters of the way through doing something the first time, you can tweak the guidance to ensure that they fully complete the task. Conventional documentation is a black box in terms of how the user interprets it.

What if you know that the user is trying to accomplish something in your product, yet is failing? Product usage data shows when users repeatedly click on a button or perform functions in an unexpected order. Imagine how that customer would feel if they see a friendly prompt in the product asking, "Can we help you with what you are trying to accomplish?" And then, a product walk-through takes them through the right steps. No frustrating call to support is required.

Assuming that you already have documentation, usage analytics can reveal some interesting measures. How often do people read help? Do certain roles use help versus others? Are new users more likely to use help than returning users? Does a new feature require documentation for its use? Are users looking at help more or less frequently after a user interface redesign? On which page were people last before clicking the help button?

It's a good idea to have a search box in your documentation and to measure commonly searched terms. I once discovered that users were searching for a term that was a synonym of a term that we used in our product—they simply didn't connect the two words. We adjusted the product to have a flexible label for this term, which increased usability and discoverability.

## MANAGING "FEATURITIS"

The best products make their users feel great. Kathy Sierra is one of my favorite authors on this topic. Her "Featuritis Curve," shown in Figure 9.1, highlights the delicate balance between helping customers become experts without confusing them to the point where they say, "I suck." If your users need extra help, they aren't feeling great—you have the chance to make them feel smart and capable. These measures are a good start. I'd also recommend having your product team spend time with support. Your support team would love the product to have more empathy for their role.

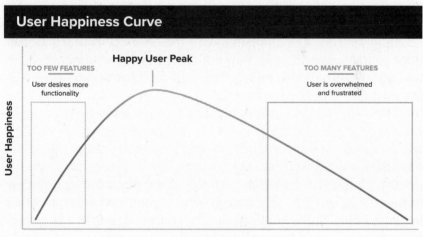

**FIGURE 9.1**   User Happiness Curve
*Source:* Pendo

No one likes to contact support, so how do we reduce the need to do so? In an ideal world, everything just works, and each user can accomplish everything they desire. However, many technology products are automating or digitizing complex processes.

## WORDS MATTER

"Words matter." This is a statement I repeat often, and it's not just because I'm writing a book right now. In nearly all aspects of life and business, each word matters, and that's why I attempt not to be cavalier in word choice. In product design, words matter a lot. We're constantly trading off clarity with brevity. Do you have an "account" or a "subscription"? Is it a "user profile" or "user settings"? The reality is that any choice you make will resonate differently with different audiences. Each user is programmed to understand certain terms based on their prior experiences, and all of our prior experiences are unique.

There are two main design solutions for this challenge. First, you can offer flexible vocabulary in your product, meaning that each customer can choose the words in the product that best resonate with them. This provides the ultimate flexibility and could even be a selling feature. The challenge with this strategy is that *if* a user does contact support, your support team may have difficulty diagnosing the issue. It also means that help documentation (especially screenshots) is nearly impossible.

The other design solution is to add tooltips pervasively throughout the product. Adding a small question mark next to labels offers the user a way to self-serve an answer if they have a simple question. For example, Restaurant365 (https://www.restaurant365.com/) offers a platform designed to help restaurant managers consolidate point-of-sale, payroll, scheduling, vendor management, and other systems into a single application. The company uses in-app guides to distribute critical release notes about their product, eliminating the need for users to navigate a help page for that information. They also use tooltips to guide users through the required fields on accounting forms, inform them of scheduled maintenance, or let them know about the effects of an architecture change.

## ONGOING CUSTOMER EDUCATION

When you launch new products or features, you have some teaching to do. Your users need some education on the underlying problem and how your product or feature solves it. They need to know why it's better than the old way, what value it brings, and how it actually works.

As you define a strategy for ongoing customer education, consider the following:

**Users learn at different speeds**: Some customers will pick things up immediately, while others may require a bit of hand-holding. Try to make it fun. But also take the time to show them the different aspects of your product.

**Meet your users where they are**: You can do this by educating customers through every channel available. Team up with your marketing and customer success organizations to get the message out via email, client platforms, press releases, articles, blogs, and webinars. Promote new products across a variety of outlets to reach as many customers as possible.

**Illustrate the functionality**: Allow users to see your product in action. You can do this with a live demo, a video, or an in-app guide letting users test things out themselves.

**Walk users through step by step**: In-app guidance allows you to highlight new features, drive preferred behavior, and provide in-context support. Contextual, personalized guidance provides help when and where it's needed, simplifies any user experience, and improves overall usability.

There is no end date when it comes to customer education. That's because the time required for a user to become proficient really isn't at all consistent. For some products, that could happen during the first use, and for others it happens through months of usage. It's important for product and customer success teams to be aware of this. Many product usage issues surface when the content and experience is designed for a specific timeline that doesn't align with how the user actually learns.

## MEASURING CUSTOMER EDUCATION

As a product manager, it's easy to fall into the trap of thinking that education isn't a product problem, and it should be owned by customer success or customer education teams. But while these teams may have primary responsibility for customer education, product teams should make sure that customers maintain proficiency in the product as new features and updates are rolled out. Without the right measurements, however, it can be difficult to keep this top of mind.

There are three key ways that product teams can evaluate the effectiveness of ongoing customer education:

**Engagement with training content**: Product teams should measure customer engagement with any content that is provided to train users on new features, especially if that content is surfaced in-app. This measure doesn't necessarily indicate the effectiveness of the content, but it shows whether users are curious and eager to learn about updates.

**Support ticket volume**: The number of support tickets associated with new features or updates can be an excellent measure of the effectiveness of ongoing education. If users cannot understand how to use new features or navigate an updated interface, they will often contact support. If significant updates are rolled out without growing support volume, the education content was likely on point.

**Long-term retention**: Customer time-to-value is an important measure for initial conversion and sale, but continued proficiency is just as important for SaaS products. If a customer is frustrated by interface changes or can no longer complete tasks as efficiently in a product, the prospect of renewal is likely to decrease. Customer education impacts this measure—retention should be considered an important downstream measure of education effectiveness.

Remember that the right amount of customer education requires a fine balance. Too much content can mean that the product isn't intuitive and can become overwhelming for users. Make sure that you are evaluating how much help is needed and communicating accordingly. There is no one-size-fits-all solution. But data-driven product managers can use these insights to help deliver excellent and continued customer education.

## Case Study: Empowering Users at Jungle Scout

More than 225,000 entrepreneurs have built businesses selling products on Amazon with help from the leading global Amazon seller software, Jungle Scout (https://www.junglescout.com/). It all started when founder Greg Mercer built a Chrome extension to track the success of products he was interested in selling on Amazon—he wanted to base decisions on data rather than gut.

Four years later, the Jungle Scout team operates a robust platform for Amazon sellers where they can conduct product research, launch new products, find and manage suppliers, and grow their businesses. During this time, Jungle Scout's growth and product expansion meant that many different customers with varying needs were using Jungle Scout at different points in their unique seller journeys. Sometimes, when users logged in for the first time, they weren't sure where to begin.

"The more customers you have, the more support tickets, so offering some level of self-service is key," says Danny Villarreal, director of customer experience at Jungle Scout. So, he brought Pendo into his organization to help launch a dedicated onboarding and training program for new users, a decision he says has given users "the kind of velocity they need to be successful."

Now when users log into the app for the first time, they see a series of in-app walk-throughs that teach them how to start using the tools. The very first gets them to what Villarreal calls "an initial aha moment"—they learn how to begin tracking products that they may be interested in selling on Amazon.

*(continued)*

(*continued*)

Jungle Scout leverages continuous user education by pointing to features that may be useful, and it includes links to relevant help articles. By enabling customers to find the help they need while using the app, Jungle Scout deflects between 16 to 21 percent of support tickets. These efforts—along with the ability to build guides in multiple languages—have also helped Jungle Scout successfully grow its business in China, where, to date, churn and refund rates are the lowest of any geographic market.

## BUILDING ON SUCCESS

After these initial wins, the Jungle Scout product team used the analytics product my company offers to learn the behaviors of its most successful users—those who have remained customers for six months or longer. Armed with six critical product usage metrics, the team built guides and tooltips to help new or less successful users replicate the actions taken by the most successful ones. Villarreal says those activities have led to a pretty massive reduction in churn. Jungle Scout users who interact with these guides are three times more likely to remain customers. "Being able to bring learning and help to users at the right points has been key, not only for us to keep them as customers, but for them to get the most out of Jungle Scout at the biggest friction points," he says.

Because users are getting a personalized onboarding experience, they see value more quickly and take advantage of the whole product. Jungle Scout says churn and refund rates continue to decline since they changed their approach. Users also need less support—Jungle Scout has experienced a notable reduction in support tickets since introducing its onboarding and user education initiatives. Ticket volume decreased by more than half in less than six months. That's meaningful time these entrepreneurs and small business owners can instead spend building and growing successful businesses on Amazon.

## SUMMARY

In short, customers of all kinds loathe asking for help. It's annoying, frustrating, and not always satisfying. Customers also get embarrassed when they ask for help—which certainly won't drive up their satisfaction scores with your product. That's why, in a product-led world, it's critical to find ways for customers to help themselves inside the product rather than relying on outside support teams. Using help metrics to identify key problems before they become widespread is essential—as is creating ways for customers to educate themselves about how to use the product and extract as much value from that experience as possible. When you build on these lessons and expand on them, you create a path not just to attract new customers, but also to retain your existing customers for life, which is the topic of the next chapter.

# CHAPTER 10

# Renew and Expand: Creating Customers for Life

In Chapter 8, we introduced the concept of delivering value, and in Chapter 9, we focused on delivering a better, more self-service experience. The results of these efforts are increased renewals and expansions across a customer base. Ideally, you want to retain 100 percent of customers and expand their usage to encompass 100 percent of your products.

For recurring revenue businesses, retaining existing customers and growing their relationship with those customers over time is likely more important than acquiring new customers. The cost to acquire a customer can be so high that customers aren't profitable until they've been a customer for a period of time.

An excellent blog post written by David Skok, where he measures the impact of churn on a SaaS business, really brings this point home. In the post, which is titled "Unlocking the Path to Negative Churn,"[1] he walks through an example where he examines the financial impact on a business by contrasting new bookings with churn rates of 2.5 percent and 5 percent a month. While those churn rates don't seem significantly different in the early days of the business, they begin to have a profound compound impact a few years later.

The goal, says Skok, is to create "negative churn" inside your business, where the revenue you gain from expansion, up-sells, and cross-sells outweighs any losses you're experiencing from churn. Over a few years, a company with a negative churn

---

[1]David Skok, "Unlocking the Path to Negative Churn," ForEntrepreneurs.com; https://www.forentrepreneurs.com/why-churn-is-critical-in-saas/

rate can generate double the monthly recurring revenue than a comparable business with even just a 2.5 percent churn rate.

So how do you create negative churn? By finding ways to generate additional revenue from users inside your product.

## UNDERSTANDING LEADING INDICATORS

The best product leaders have a strong understanding of what's driving positive business outcomes. Specifically, they know which usage patterns correlate to account growth and renewal. By identifying leading indicators at your business, you'll have the insight necessary to nudge people toward the features and behaviors that have led their peers to expanded usage.

## MEASURING RETENTION OVER TIME

Equally important is measuring retention over time. This is how you know if your onboarding efforts are yielding just temporary changes in user behavior or habits that stick. Think of the applications you use regularly. There are probably a few in your life and work around which you've truly built habits and rituals—the things you do every morning over coffee or every Sunday evening as you prepare for the work week ahead. For me, one application that I use regularly and couldn't imagine giving up is 15Five (https://www.15five.com/), a performance management platform that my company uses to keep our teams on the same page. It measures employee happiness, their priorities, their accomplishments, and any blockers to their progress. We use it to create and maintain alignment across our company.

If you looked at our usage trends in 15Five over time, you'd see a steady week-over-week trend—a signal of a healthy and happy customer. But there are probably other applications that would reveal a very different trend: a spike in initial usage followed by substantial decay over time. This should signal something else entirely—user habits that never quite took root. Understanding the retention of user cohorts allows you to answer the ever-important question: How much would my customers care if they no longer had access to my product? Declining retention is generally a signal that they may not answer this question the way you'd like them to.

But knowing whether or not you're retaining users isn't enough. For this insight to be actionable, you'll want to understand why or why not. This requires a different lens into retention—one that looks at individual features inside your product. With this insight, you can start to understand which features are sticky and which ones are fleeting in their usefulness to your customers.

The job of onboarding never ends. It's about understanding what your users are trying to achieve with your application and continuously fulfilling these needs over time. And it should be seen as more than just satisfying the first-use experience. These first impressions matter a lot to be sure, but once you've welcomed new users into your application, you need to be sure they're coming back for more. The ones who don't come back are forever customers at risk.

## Case Study: Building Customer Health Scores

Do you know the difference between the customers who are thriving on your application and those who are unhealthy? That can be an especially difficult question to answer as your organization scales. If you have hundreds, or even thousands of customers, how will you identify the unhealthy ones?

This was an issue that Rapid7 (https://www.rapid7.com/), a cybersecurity firm with multiple offices around the globe, needed to confront. The more customers they onboarded, the larger their blind spot around customer health became. To address this problem head-on, they made the decision to create a customer health score against which all customers could be quickly and easily measured.

*(continued)*

(*continued*)

## GETTING STARTED: HEALTH SCORE DATA BINGO

When the Rapid7 team took on the customer health score project, they quickly discovered that building this metric would require a multi-departmental effort. The first step was to establish a steering committee for the initiative, which included team members from multiple departments, including product, marketing, and customer success.

Next, the team needed to select the data points that should be included in the CHS metric. The first exercise the team tried was "Health Score Data Bingo," which was basically a sticky note session where they put every metric they could think of on a whiteboard. Then they winnowed down and prioritized the metrics. They ended up breaking their list of numbers down into "initial," "medium-term," and "long-term" categories, based on how quickly they felt they could incorporate each metric into their overall customer health score model. Here's the breakdown:

### Initial

- Product adoption
- Support experience
- Purchasing behavior

### Medium-term

- CSM input
- CSM interactions
- NPS

### Long-term

- IT ecosystem
- Security maturity
- Product certifications

## A CUSTOMER HEALTH SCORE MODEL

For their initial pass at a customer health score, the steering committee decided to start simple and include only their "initial" metrics in the model. Over time, they planned to incorporate additional data points in the overall score. Rapid7's first customer health score was an amalgam of the following: product adoption (40%), support experience (35%), and purchasing behavior (25%). If data on customer success interactions was available, that accounted for 35 percent of the score in place of support experience.

Each of these three components was itself a mashup of multiple data points. For example, the support experience piece of Rapid7's CHS score included stats like NPS, time to close, and number of escalations. And the purchasing behavior component included the number of products, number of renewals, and lost versus open opportunities.

Based on their score, a customer would be classified as "very unhealthy," "unhealthy," "neutral," "healthy," or "very healthy." Plans of action would then be put into place according to that score, with unhealthy customers receiving more attention than healthy ones.

## PUTTING CUSTOMER SCORES INTO ACTION

The customer health score framework they put in place now allows Rapid7 to identify unhealthy customers easily and "treat" them accordingly. It also makes prioritization much easier, with the less healthy customers moving to the top of the list. Finally, the team can see how a customer's score is trending over time. Hopefully, unhealthy customers move toward health over time, and healthy customers stay that way. If not, the team can quickly address the issue.

Since Rapid7's initial adoption of a customer health score, they've come away with some key insights. For one, they've discovered that some unhealthy customers may already be lost. At

*(continued)*

(*continued*)

a certain point, no amount of additional support will bring them back to health. Second, healthy customers are the best cross-sell candidates. They're the most likely to buy more of your product. Neutral customers, however, are where you should spend the greatest amount of time. These customers are satisfied but "untapped." With a little extra attention, they can become your company's biggest advocates. Finally, creating a customer health score model requires a lot of trial and error. If your team wants to build one, just start doing it and iterate as you go.

One of the powerful aspects about health scores is that they enable you to take a range of variables and data points and coalesce them into a single score that helps you prioritize where to spend your time with a customer while better understanding what risks you face with them.

That's especially true when you use more of a visual indicator, like a health score that shows green for healthy, yellow as an early warning, or red as an immediate threat. With this color code as your guide, you immediately know where you need to spend time and energy to save customers you might be in danger of losing.

The catch with a health score is to make sure that you are measuring the true signals of your customer's health and not just noise. As with any score, the better the data is going into it, the better the outcome will be coming out.

The challenge with maintaining an accurate health score over time, therefore, is ensuring that the right data is being used to calculate it. For example, when we started Pendo, we gave our customers the power to slice and dice customer data arbitrarily, any way they wanted to. Later on, we added a new feature to our software called "Segments," which helped simplify that process of slicing and dicing data. When we created our customer health score, one of the data points we used was how often customers were using the segment feature. What we didn't recognize, of course, was that we still had some customers using the older version of our software. They weren't aware of the new feature—or didn't have access to it—so they were flashing up with red health scores even if they were, in fact, happy customers.

What we learned is that a health score is a living and breathing thing, and it needs to reflect the current state of how your customers are using your product.

The value of health scores also extends just beyond a customer management use case. If customers are unhappy, it's unlikely that it's the fault of customer management. It's a product problem—which is why there is tremendous value in having product team members intimately involved with customer health scoring and analyzing usage patterns on the journey to create better products that, over time, create happier customers.

## RETENTION

So, what's the purpose of health scores? Retention. The cost to acquire a customer can be substantial. We don't want to lose those customers. Yet we can't spend our time (despite our best efforts) with every single customer. Health scores are essentially a warning sign—an indicator of where to spend time. You should be able to ignore green customers to focus on red ones.

Now that we know which customers to focus on, what should we do? First, we can leverage data to inform our interactions with the customer. Tell them where they are missing out on opportunities to get more value from using our product. You can also use data to show how other customers use your products, or even share examples of what certain customers are doing well, which can inspire other users to follow suit.

Similarly, we can leverage health scores to automate in-application interactions. For example, messaging low-usage customers with suggestions for how they might benefit from increasing their use of the product can deliver more value to the customer prior to engaging them in a conversation about renewing.

## CROSS-SELL/UPSELL

Once you have established a strong product-led retention strategy, you've opened up the possibilities to grow your business by helping existing users do more inside your product. Sometimes this is called "land and expand." This is the mantra for most subscription businesses, but it applies to just about any kind of business model. You want to get customers hooked on your products by delivering something specific and valuable. Then, you can find ways to expand the relationship. Cross-selling, simply defined, is selling customers different products. Up-selling is selling them more—amount or capabilities—of the same product. A product could notice that you are at the limit of what you've purchased and automatically prompt you to purchase more. Or a product could prompt an engaged and happy user to use advanced capabilities that could deliver increased value. To build these prompts, you need to understand what features might resonate most with your users. Intuit offers a prime example—users of its Quicken software receive a message around tax time letting them know how easily Quicken integrates with another Intuit product, TurboTax, as a way to prompt the user to purchase that product as well. It's all with an eye on giving that customer value in return for their investment.

## SUMMARY

We hear a lot of organizations express a desire to create "customers for life." But what does that really mean—and how do you do it? In this chapter, we talked about how your product is a critical piece of machinery that cannot just attract customers but also retain them over the long haul. To understand how to retain customers, you need to shift your thinking by looking at leading indicators like heath scores, which reflect how satisfied your customers really are. When you have that kind of data-driven insight, you've opened a path to finding additional ways to engage and retain your customer base—like cross-selling and up-selling them the full range of your product offering. But I'd be remiss not to cover another driver of happy customers for life—you also must continue to evolve and reimagine your product so that your customer continues to gain value. We'll turn to that challenge in the third section of the book, in which we discuss a new way of delivering products in a product-led world.

# Three

# A New Way of Delivering Product

To tackle the topics that we covered in the first two sections of this book well, you need a product delivery strategy. And that requires collaboration across customers, your own teams, and within your product team. With the help of data and a focus on delivering on the promise of a great customer experience, product-led organizations must also learn how to rethink their approach to designing and delivering new products and features, which is the focus of this third section of the book.

Companies need to be good listeners in the digital age, and that requires a new set of skills. It means listening to customers as they are using your product and guiding them to better results. It means positive outcomes, including understanding the levers of engagement and driving overall adoption.

Product management as a discipline was born out of Procter & Gamble, a multinational consumer packaged goods company. While there's been quite a bit of adaptation of the discipline to account for technology, and even software, it's still relatively immature. Rapid advances in business models, engineering practices, and technology have forced product management to evolve.

The product-led movement is the latest disruptor to our conventional models of managing products. It challenges how we organize our teams, communicate with customers, and manage feedback. Conventional models aren't sufficient to keep up with the rapid pace of change and the volume of data that we now have at our disposal.

Another aspect of this is measuring the ROI of your development activities by knowing what is and what is not being used in your product (and making the decision to retire those features). This extends to your planned functionality as well, as you can gain data necessary to improve prioritization of your roadmap.

In short, your efforts are focused on what is working because you actually have the information, in many cases for the first time, from your customer. You are both improving their use of your product and making better decisions about your resources—continuously.

# CHAPTER 11

# Product-led Design

**B**ack in Chapter 3, I shared a story of how, early in my career, I learned to use techniques like think-aloud studies to elicit feedback from users on how to improve their experience. Teams had robust usability labs behind two-way mirrors to watch users interact with software. Back then, design was a very heavy process. Today, design is more dynamic and fluid.

## VALIDATE THE USER EXPERIENCE EARLY

There's a temptation for product owners to jump in and start building the product idea that they sketched out on a napkin with a customer over drinks. Not a great idea.

The second they start formalizing plans and resources to develop a minimum viable product (MVP), they lock themselves into a path that limits their ability to apply divergent thinking. Additionally, the high mental overhead of a formal development project can easily shift thinking to developer resourcing, requirement specs, and sprint planning instead of capturing the opportunity to nail the customer experience up front.

Teams need to give themselves permission to work together on ideation exercises—like storyboarding and mind mapping—and then flesh out ideas with simple low-fidelity prototypes that show how product concepts and screens flow together. What follows are more detailed prototypes that fully articulate the vision—they look, feel, and work in a way that is indistinguishable from the final vision of the product. Every click, tap, and swipe should be as intended.

Today, prototypes have reached higher fidelity. It's possible to add animations, micro-interactions, and hover states—all the little nuances that make the product what it is. This is important for gathering more meaningful feedback and for getting designers and developers in full alignment so that the product that ships is the product that was designed. In many cases, you can have a user try an entire product that's a mocked-up experience. This generates feedback early enough to save potentially hours of time building something that may not be the optimal solution.

An approach developed by the investment group GV is called a five-day "sprint."[1] The idea is to address critical business issues with your customers by taking an idea through design, prototyping, and testing to develop a working prototype. Rather than spending weeks, months, or longer in an infinite feedback loop, working together with your customers in a sprint is a way to launch a minimum viable product in just a week.

All of these steps are critical to ensuring that not a single line of code is written until the product direction is validated by and articulated to your users.

## CROSS-FUNCTIONAL COLLABORATION

Innovative design is not a discrete service, and it doesn't happen in a silo. It's a highly collaborative process of continuous prototyping and iteration, and it's dependent on getting buy-in from as many diverse viewpoints as possible, as early as possible.

Diverse internal and external feedback has two major advantages. It takes into consideration corner-cases of product use, creating a more comprehensive view of the customer, and it helps product teams ship the right product the first time and focus on iteration—not "back to the drawing board" repetition. For example, say that you want to understand areas of friction and experiment with some solutions (see the sections on identifying and removing friction in Chapter 8). Testing with users who have

---

[1] GV website: https://www.gv.com/sprint/

actually experienced this friction tends to generate better insights. However, sometimes those users create workarounds or habits that make them immune to areas of minor friction that could cause major issues for novice users. Take onboarding as a specific case. By definition, existing users are onboard, so they likely aren't a good test audience for your re-designed onboarding process.

Bring customers into the fold for these discussions. Include developers at every step. Perhaps having your development team watch a customer interact with a prototype and talk out loud might create more of an emotional connection with the user. Share your plans with marketing and sales. Get executive buy-in early. Critical insight can come from anywhere, at any moment, so look for it early. When everyone is aligned on the vision from the start, better products ship faster at the end.

## OPERATIONALIZING DESIGN AT SCALE

*Design debt* happens when there is an overabundance of non-reusable and inconsistent styles and conventions in your product—and the interest to pay on that debt is the impossible task of maintaining the mess. Over time, the accumulation of this debt becomes a great weight that slows growth.

Having operational maturity in a design practice reduces this debt and pays huge dividends across the product development life-cycle. It can double the speed of design and iteration and keep the customer experience from looking disjointed. One important step to achieving this level of maturity is the adoption of a design system.

A *design system* creates a single source of truth, a design language in which everyone is instantly fluent and that can quickly and easily be pulled into designs, prototypes, and directly into code. It reduces design debt, accelerates the design process, and builds bridges between teams working in concert to bring products to life. Unfortunately, this is an area in which many product teams under-invest. That underinvestment often leads to systems that aren't universally adopted and therefore have almost no value. Adoption is truly paramount to having a consistent design and aligned team.

It's important to consider three audiences when operationalizing design and driving system adoption:

**Designers**: Does it operationalize design in the tools and workflow that designers already use and create a common language around which it's easy to align?

**Developers**: Does it make that design language easily accessible to developers through an API?

**Other stakeholders**: Does it showcase a single source of design truth that's accessible to every facet of the organization (and even externally)?

A good design system will also gracefully separate these different audiences through strong access control, versioning, and data protection in order to keep the integrity of your design language intact.

Today's most disruptive and beloved digital products are created by design teams that consider the customer at every step of their process. They understand their customer's problem, understand how others in or outside of their organization understand that problem, and then collaborate on a vision that solves it best. When everyone is all-in on the vision, every decision that follows is informed by a deeply rooted organizational empathy. Once that why is embraced, their next great product is only a few whats and hows away.

## SUMMARY

The whole approach of how we design products has changed forever. Gone are the days when product managers could rely solely on their gut instinct and experience to make decisions about what users want. Today, we need to embrace Agile thinking when it comes to design, where we prioritize speed in prototyping and collaboration across teams to deliver the most impactful product designs that address a customer's pain. In the next chapter, we'll talk about how those same principles can be applied as we rethink how we launch products and drive adoption among users.

# CHAPTER 12

# Launching and Driving Adoption

I've been developing software for most of my life. I've also started three companies from scratch. When it comes to launching software and getting users to adopt it, there are a couple of formative lessons I've learned from those experiences from which you can also benefit. In short, we can launch products much more strategically today than we did in the past.

The first big lesson I've learned is that with the advent of cloud-based software, or SaaS, you can get changes in front of users instantly. This is incredibly valuable, especially because hardware can get stupid fairly quickly when it doesn't have the latest software powering it. The real payoff from having faster release cycles is that we can collect feedback more frequently, which is how we ensure that products are best aligned to customer needs. This also happens to be the primary goal of Agile.

The second lesson I can share relates to how the traditional approach to delivering software has changed. We used to conceive the product, then engineer and build it, and then ship it to the end user as a serialized "waterfall" progression. But this approach was flawed. In the companies I ran, we baked too many assumptions into the product up front, which made it difficult to iterate and change over time.

In other words, we shipped software based on outdated requirements. Then, by the time our product was released, our customers had new requirements that our release failed to cover. Even worse, we may have misunderstood their requirements all along. At that point, we lost the chance to meet our customers' needs, and we had to tell them that it would take another 12 to 18 months to correct our mistake. Of course, then it becomes a vicious cycle.

When I started in this business, we were still shipping CDs and boxes and writing books filled with documentation. It was common for companies to have these giant dusty credenzas whose only purpose was to store all of the outdated manuals they had accumulated over the years. I know that this sounds comically old fashioned, but it wasn't that long ago that this was common practice. In those days, software companies had to conceive of big new feature sets to entice users to make the trip to a CompUSA to buy the latest version of the software.

Updating software is often painful for many users. When I was head of products at a large software company, we would ship out big feature releases only to spend days answering angry calls from customers complaining about the changes. Even though we'd conducted educational webinars and written dozens of blogs to help prepare them for the upcoming changes, people still freaked out.

We'd then talk to our engineers and tell them that we needed to slow down the number of changes in the product. But, as you might already know, this is exactly the opposite of the engineering mindset. Engineers are never satisfied with what they've just shipped—they want to make more improvements, not less. Since then, the way we ship software has changed. We could no longer continue to ship into a vacuum and expect customers to adopt our products.

I started my latest company, Pendo, as a way to overcome these challenges. We wanted to help product teams build a sticky product right from the start, allowing the product to pull the business rather than having the business try to force-feed the product to customers—in other words, getting the product right and letting the business flow from there.

New products, and even new features, have a lifecycle. There's the coding, testing, and deploying process. But that's just the building phase. It's often downplayed how much of the work can take place post deployment. The next phases include limited release, launch, growth, and death. Yes, nearly every product or feature dies at some point. Typically, we call this "sunsetting," which is simply a euphemism for death. During each phase, there are different goals and different measures to consider.

During limited release and launch, I'm measuring a few distinct things:

* Who's trying it?
* Does it deliver on the intended value to those users?

Of course, not all products or features are intended for continual use, so the measure of intended value highly depends on the product or feature's intent. More significantly, "who" matters a lot in the launch phase. In Geoffrey Moore's famous framework he introduced in *Crossing the Chasm* (Collins Business Essentials, 2014), he separated the market into Innovators, Early Adopters, Early Majority, Late Majority, and Laggards. So, in the launch period, I'm specifically measuring how my innovators and early adopters use the new product, and I'm soliciting qualitative feedback to measure their first impressions. Given that early adopters are accustomed to using early products, their expectations are realistic and typically a good sign of future success.

## CONTROLLED ROLLOUT

We have always had this notion in software that we can conduct a controlled rollout of things. We can test the new product or features and then roll them out to everyone—what is known as "generally available" or GA in tech.

The general idea is to put an early version of the product out in advance as a way to collect feedback, iterate, and then decide when it will be ready to roll out to the entire GA customer base. We typically release several different versions of the software to gauge its readiness, starting with "alpha," which implies a super-early version of something, and "beta," which is when we let people bang on the thing and tell us how well it's working. You also might see terms like "Limited Beta" or "Open Beta," which indicate how many people might be given access to that product. (Another term, "gamma," is used rarely, if at all.)

The idea is to launch a product that's not fully baked and then give certain users the opportunity to help evolve it—this gives them some sense of control and ownership over helping you make it a success. In some cases, products might stay in a beta release for years. Google's beta version of Gmail, for example, launched in 2004. But it remained in beta until 2009, when the GA version was officially released.

Your beta customers are the best—they love you and you love them. These are the folks who love letting you know about any bugs they find.

Today it's rare to release something that hasn't been used by early users—internal or external. Some companies have entire programs around alpha or beta releases. Regardless of the sophistication, these are important gates in the process for general availability. Typically, the goal of these early releases is to gauge readiness. Is this ready for prime time?

Product features begin as experiments. Variations are rolled out to user segments or sample groups, and the impact is measured against product metrics. As features refine, they are progressively rolled out to larger and larger groups of users who are then notified of updates and educated on new functionality. Product teams now roll out updates as a series of running experiments with more and more users invited as functionality hardens and improves.

Engineering agility has increased by orders of magnitude every five years, almost like Moore's law, which refers to the rate at which computing speed will increase. Two decades ago, it took Microsoft two years to ship Windows XP. Since then, the industry norm is shipping software every six months, quarter, month, week, and now every day. The technologies enabling this revolution are well known: cloud, continuous integration (CI), and continuous delivery (CD), to name a few. If the trend holds, in another five years, the average engineering team will be doing dozens of daily deploys.

Beyond engineering, Agile development has reshaped product management, moving it away from waterfall releases to a faster cadence. Minimum viable features are shipped early and followed by a rapid iteration cycle based on continuous customer feedback.

Not that long ago, design was a pursuit in "making it pretty." Today, design thinking and practices permeate every step of bringing products to market. Companies like Airbnb, Facebook, Netflix, and Amazon have reshaped entire industries by employing design-forward practices that make them look almost clairvoyant as they release every new version of their product.

As disruptors set the tone, everyone from startups to established Fortune 500 enterprises are now building dynamic, inclusive, and scalable design practices. While Agile defines a world of rapid iteration during the development phase, an increasing number of product teams are applying an Agile approach to the design phase too, where they can iterate faster and with even fewer constraints. It's how the best companies in the world are delivering customer experiences that are a generational leap over anything that came before.

## DEATH OF THE SOFTWARE RELEASE

As our software development processes have evolved, we've mostly said goodbye to the idea of defined product versions. Many modern product delivery teams are taking this a step further—even the concept of a "product release" is starting to fade. Instead, our products are becoming a fluid, rapidly evolving set of features, assembled uniquely for any given user.

Twenty-five years ago, a new release of a software product was a notable event. This is still the case for a few types of software—operating systems being the most notable—but for most of the software products that we use on a daily basis, the concept of a version has faded away. What version of Google Maps are you using these days? How about Facebook? Twitter? As far as the end-user is concerned, there is no version, just whatever is current.

The rise of Agile software methodologies and associated practices such as continuous delivery has allowed software teams to tighten up software delivery cycles dramatically. Products that were once released every few months are now released every few days. In parallel, the growing capabilities of the web as a platform has moved many products off of the desktop and into the browser. This has greatly reduced the friction involved in releasing a new version of a product. Product management no longer must worry about broad sweeping release days—days controlled by engineering with late-night release trains, and several on-call engineers from across different functions. Instead, for many product delivery organizations, it has become the norm for any change to be managed by feature flags. Product changes are no longer "launched" or "released"—they are incrementally rolled out.

## THE NECESSARY ADOPTION OF FEATURE FLAGS

*Feature flags*, where you can turn features on and off during a release, can also be components of alpha and beta tests. You can use these to roll out certain features to a limited set of customers as a way to test things on a more gradual scale.

If you're not familiar with feature flags, think of them as a way to deploy a piece of code in production while restricting access to only a subset of users. This service is controlled dynamically outside of the code, not requiring engineering resources to make a change.

Tesla is an example of a company that uses feature flags. As a customer, you can automatically opt into using the latest and greatest software in your vehicle, or you can choose to be a slower adopter. If you want to let other users test those features before you're ready, or if you're someone who doesn't like your cheese being moved, you have that option to wait.

A related technique is to give users the ability to roll back an update—a "go back" button of sorts—which again gives them control over their experience. This approach also has the added advantage of giving you, the software builder, lots of actionable information on what your users like or dislike. Once you have enough users who don't opt to roll back, for example, you know you've got it down.

For some users, especially businesses, constantly adding new features can be disruptive. If you're running your e-commerce business on an open source Linux operating system, for instance, which is constantly being updated by an army of volunteer hackers around the world, you might like to have the ability to control when and how those updates are implemented. But that's exactly the business model employed by a company like Red Hat. Businesses pay Red Hat to curate their version of Linux, where it's tested and rolled out in a controlled fashion that doesn't disrupt their day-to-day operations. There is a ton of value in using this approach.

Feature flags have a widespread number of use cases across both the product and engineering teams. Most specifically, for product management, feature flags provide the ability to do the following:

**Test in production**: Feature flags allow teams to perform functional and performance tests directly in production with a subset of customers. This is a secure and performant way of understanding how a new feature will scale with customers.

**Safely roll out new functionality**: By having a feature behind a flag, product managers can roll it out to subsets of customers or remove it from all customers if it is causing problems for the customer experience. This idea of "killing" a feature is better than having to depend on engineering to push an emergency fix or a code rollback.

**Take a measured approach to product management**: Rolling out a change involves monitoring the impact of that change. As feature flagging has moved into the domain of product management, product managers have focused their measurement on higher-level business key performance indicators (KPIs): active users, conversion rates, business transactions per hour, and so forth.

You can also conduct tests with a random sample of customers. You might, for instance, create a control group using 10 percent of your customers chosen at random. That way you can help identify issues, and roll back the version, with just 10 percent of your customers versus 100 percent of them.

The online craft marketplace Etsy (https://www.etsy.com/) is famous for shipping multiple updates every day—sometimes as many as 50 updates in a single day. They track each of these updates carefully. If any one of those changes spikes user activity in a negative way, they automatically roll back the change.

There is a downside to feature flags that you have to keep in mind. Consider what happens if every one of your users has a different set of flags turned on. How does your support team know which flag is active when someone calls with a problem? Or how do you even write documentation for your product based on multiple combinations of flags that might be turned on or off?

Maintaining code that has too many feature flags can also become unsustainable and unmanageable. Every time you want to add a new feature, it might take forever because there are too many flags to work around—something we call "flag debt." At some point, you need to go back and start removing some of your old flags.

The emerging practice of product experimentation is enabled by the feature flag and paired with the telemetry to measure the impact of these features on customer experience.

## RISE OF PRODUCT EXPERIMENTATION

Many have turned to online controlled experiments as the optimal way to deliver valuable software rapidly. These product experimentation platforms provide clarity and help product teams measure the impact of product development on the customer experience.

In an experiment enabled by the use of feature flags, users are randomly assigned to treatment and control groups. The treatment group is given access to a feature; the control is not. Product instrumentation captures metrics (or KPIs) for users, and a statistical engine measures any difference in metrics between treatment and control to determine if the feature caused—not just correlated with—a change in the team's metrics. The change in the team's metrics, or those of an unrelated team, could be good or bad, intended or unintended. Armed with this data, product and engineering teams can continue the release to more users, iterate on its functionality, or scrap the idea. Thus, only the valuable ideas survive.

Experimentation is not a novel idea. Most popular consumer products—the likes of Google, Facebook, or Netflix—run experiments regularly. It is through experimentation that product management organizations are able to truly measure the impact of their development efforts on customer experience.

But there's another angle to explore if you operate in the business-to-business, or B2B, world of software. We've found that you can actually charge some customers more money for giving them access to new features. They're willing to pay for the privilege of seeing what's cooking in the labs and then helping to shape it. They enjoy having some degree of control and influence over the creative process, which is a benefit they're willing to pay for.

## FEATURE AWARENESS AND ADOPTION

Product teams are naturally excited when they prepare to roll out a major new feature. In a perfect world, that feature is immediately and enthusiastically adopted by every customer. In reality, that's rarely the case. Feature adoption tends to be sporadic, and a lot of teams don't have visibility into how their product is used to truly understand how widely a feature is adopted.

Every product team wants to build features that provide value to customers, but doing so requires effective customer feedback, appropriate measurements, and an ability to drive awareness rapidly around new updates.

But the way we educate and enable users has to evolve. You can't just rely on shipping some documentation along with the software anymore. You have to think differently about it. That's why you may be greeted with a guided tour of new features when you open an app on your phone or a pop-up message when you hover over a new button.

Figuring out how to tell people when you have a new feature becomes a big challenge due to the sheer number of stakeholders involved. On one hand, you have your customers. On another, you have your internal support team. You don't want to roll out a bunch of new features without educating customers about the newest changes, or you'll soon get a bunch of help desk tickets about issues the support team didn't even know existed.

There are a couple of different philosophies that can come into play here. If you're Etsy, and you're releasing updates 50 times a day, you can't announce each and every one of those. It simply doesn't scale.

Some companies choose to take a blended approach. They might make an announcement on social media for every change, but then they follow with a quarterly summary to customers explaining what changes they made over those three months.

But the best way to tackle announcements is to place them directly in your app. An effective approach can be to add a new button or badge that flashes or glows when updates have been made, triggering users to click or hover. This way, you avoid interrupting users but still give them the chance to learn what changes have been made. Once they click the button, the flash or glow goes away.

## WHY PRODUCT SUCCESS DEPENDS ON FEATURE ADOPTION

We've talked a lot about the shift to subscription-based software licensing, where many software products are purchased over and over again—sometimes as frequently as every month—as customers renew their subscriptions. Each and every renewal is contingent on customers perceiving and receiving ongoing value from the software, which means that each new product feature presents an opportunity for additive value if customers are aware of and actively using it.

Unused features, however, can have an adverse effect. This is why product teams are increasingly focused on overall product adoption. Every piece of a product that isn't used represents something a customer is paying for but not realizing value from. Underuse lowers perceived value and ultimately a customer's willingness to pay for a product.

### Measuring Feature Adoption

On the surface, it seems simple enough to measure feature adoption: Are customers using the feature or not? But usage may not be the best benchmark for adoption. Consider the following scenarios. Software company A releases an update and publicizes the update broadly to the current user base. As a result, over 40 percent of their users use the feature over the next week. However, a week later almost none of them continue to use the feature. Software company B also releases and publicizes a new feature. Only a tiny percentage of users pick up the feature, but they enthusiastically continue to use it.

Both scenarios are examples of feature adoption, but neither would be judged particularly successful. Neither feature provided significant ongoing value to customers. When measuring feature adoption, companies should consider the following dimensions:

**Breadth of adoption**: How widely has a feature been adopted across the user base or targeted user segment? Has the feature been used by a majority of the targeted users, or only a small percentage? Looking at the breadth of adoption shows the initial appeal of the new feature.

**Time to adopt**: How long does it take for users to begin using a new feature? When learning about a feature, do users immediately try it out, or do they wait several days or weeks? Looking at adoption time provides input into motivation. The more quickly a feature is adopted, the more likely it addresses a significant customer pain or usability problem.

**Duration of adoption**: How long do users continue to use a feature after learning about it? Do they try it out a few times or continue to use it regularly? This is an important measurement, as it helps to show whether a feature is providing any real value beyond its initial novelty.

What constitutes successful adoption across these three dimensions is obviously going to vary from use case to use case, but it's important to consider all three when assessing the outcome of any feature release.

## Promoting Feature Launches

New software features will never see significant adoption if the user base doesn't know about them. So, the announcement and discovery process are also important parts of driving adoption. There's no "one size fits all" way to announce features, but there are a couple of considerations that can help to shape the strategy. The first one is relevance. Users are much more likely to respond to announcements that matter to them. Software applications—especially business software applications—have diverse user bases with different roles, maturity, and technical proficiency. Very few features are deeply relevant to all users. Therefore, the announcement approach should be tailored to the most appropriate user segments. Whether a new feature is relevant to prospective customers in addition to the current user base can also shape the announcement strategy.

The second consideration is desired action. What should users do upon reading the announcement? Try it out? Read documentation about how to use it? Provide feedback? The desired next action can also have an impact on the best way to announce a new feature. In many cases, the product itself can provide a powerful channel for new feature announcements. Delivering feature announcements or promotions in the form of in-app modals or tooltips ensures that the announcement reaches users at a highly relevant time (when they're using the product). A best practice is to segment the announcements for different groups of users for even greater relevance.

Often, the primary next action for users is to try the feature. If the announcement is served directly in the product, there's nothing stopping the user from trying it out. With email or blog announcements, users must either immediately log in to the product to try out the feature or attempt to remember the announcement the next time they use the product.

## Improving Feature Adoption

Increasing feature adoption ultimately comes down to the value that each feature delivers. But understanding that value requires clear insight. To understand adoption, product teams should measure the breadth, time, and duration of feature adoption, and they must pair those metrics with direct user feedback about specific features.

Discoverability also plays an outsized role in feature adoption. By leveraging the right promotion strategy, product teams can ensure that highly actionable announcements reach the users for whom they will be the most valuable.

Effective measurement will help product teams understand the extent to which new features are adopted, but it certainly won't tell them why or what users really think about a particular feature. The only way to collect this important information is to ask for it. Look for opportunities to collect feedback when users are interacting with a new feature for the first few times. Some companies prefer open-ended feedback, while others use a number scale or yes/no questions to gather a baseline on perceived user value.

## GOAL SETTING AND TRACKING

After the work is done and the dust settled, you need to check back in on your goal to see how you did. Did you hit it? Were you even close? Was the goal the right goal? It doesn't really matter how you articulated the goal. What matters is that you check back in with it and document what you've learned. Maybe you failed miserably on achieving the intended goal. Maybe you completely missed something in your original thesis. That's OK (well, it should be OK). The key is to incorporate what you've learned into the model, framework, or template. Then, do better next time. And this requires a lot of discipline. I see most teams set goals, work hard, ship something, and move on to the next project. I would contend that you're not actually done with a given piece of work until you've intentionally decided whether to finish the work or not. In the past, I've created a feature or epic Kanban board that encapsulates this broader process.

In this process, there is an explicit phase to collect evidence or data. During this period, the intent is to measure and iterate on the software. Only when you've been truly validated are you near a true completion state and ready to celebrate with champagne and red Solo cups.

## SUMMARY

In this chapter, we covered how to launch your products successfully and ensure that customers use them. We'll take things in a dramatically different direction in the next chapter when we look at how product-led companies decide when it's actually time to retire features and products.

# CHAPTER 13

# The Art of Letting Go

I t is said that "all good things come to an end," and that can apply to products and features. It's important not to grow too emotionally attached to the things you've built. If something has outlived its usefulness, it's absolutely better to remove it. There are always going to be new and better ways of doing things. But if your code is old and taking up space—while also creating defects—you eventually have to deal with that code debt. There's also the additional factor of cluttering the user interface. Each additional capability requires maintenance and training, and it adds complexity to the user experience. In other words, less is actually more because extra complexity and bloat have real consequences. Brian Crofts, our chief product officer at Pendo, likes to say that the role of product management is not eliminating, but slowing the inexorable creep of complexity. Therefore, one of the best things a product manager can do is retire features that aren't being used or adding value. But you can't do this without deep insight into user behavior and sentiment. Retiring features with this insight is powerful; retiring features without it is dangerous.

You can start by talking with your engineering team about potential features to kill. I'm sometimes approached by engineers who absolutely hate a piece of code. They may be embarrassed by it, or perhaps the engineer who wrote it is long gone, and every time it's touched, something unintended breaks that causes the team to pad estimates. But the most important insights come from the remaining users. Once you understand the remaining users and customers, you can start to devise a transition plan.

## GRACEFUL REDUCTION

Removing code is one of the most powerful things that you can do as a product person. Less is always more, and your engineers will love you for it. Your customers will, too.

A super counterintuitive aspect of building software is that people don't brag about getting rid of things. People get compensated for adding features—not removing them. But keeping old features is actually more expensive and time consuming than you might think. It's taking up valuable space and capacity. Rather than trying to explain the rationale to your sales team for why you should keep an old feature, you would be better served to just to get rid of it. If a feature isn't valuable, it's time to kill it.

There are many techniques to go about doing this.

### Test the Pain

One lesson I've learned is that if you actually ask your users if you should remove a feature, they will inevitably say "no." People don't like change—even if it's a feature that they aren't actually using, as you recognize from your metrics. One solution, therefore, is just to remove the feature and see how badly people yell and scream about it. That's a pretty useful and interesting tactic that marries analytics with intuition.

In Pendo's early days as a startup, we would get rid of something in the UI and then wait to see what happened.

Thanks to our ability to measure usage, process feedback, and analyze sentiment, we don't have to guess anymore. We have tools like Pendo to help us make decisions informed by data. If nobody complained or noticed, we knew we were safe. Maybe this is an extreme example, but we trusted the fact that we wouldn't lose customers because of one missing feature.

You can also use your metrics as a guide for removing features. If you see that, say, a feature is popular with your small business customers but completely ignored by your large company users, that tells you something valuable. If your goal is to attract larger companies, you'll need to develop different capabilities.

## Check Your Vision

As you consider features to remove, think about whether they're part of your past or part of your future. If you're targeting more enterprise customers going forward, then that feature used by your small company users might be a good candidate for removal.

Another approach is to engage your customers in a conversation. Don't ask them a question like, "What do you think about this feature?" Rather, ask them something like, "If you didn't have this feature, what would you do instead?" The goal here is to understand their pain better to see how that feature actually solves it.

You can then work with your customer to develop a solution for their problem that also allows you to remove the feature. You might, for instance, show them a screenshot or a mock-up of a replacement solution. Granted, this approach might take a lot of work. But ideally you are giving them a better solution—a carrot that is both better and faster for them.

Another goal when it comes to removing features is to garner empathy from your customers. You might stress how hard it is for your team to support this feature or point out its bugs. Ultimately, you're trying to assure your customer that you are trying to develop a better solution for their pain, even though it might take some retraining and learning new habits to get there.

## OVERCOMING THE CHALLENGES OF REWRITES

Rewriting software is a very difficult process. Why? Because your "new" thing is competing against the features of your "old" thing. The word your team will be fighting is "parity." There may be an expectation of parity from customers or executives about the balance of the old and new, regardless of whether they understand the challenge of reimplementing years of institutional decisions/knowledge. In many cases, the product manager working on the rewrite is new to the area of the product, and the original product manager may no longer be with the company.

It can be difficult to get users to move beyond the legacy of those old features that you're trying to move away from.

A great article written by tech entrepreneur Herb Caudill goes into great detail about the challenges that companies face when it comes time to rewrite their software. In his piece "Lessons from 6 Software Rewriting Stories," Caudill explores some of the strategies that companies have used to ease their way through the process of rewriting old software.[1]

Caudill points to a famous quote by tech entrepreneur, Joel Spolsky, who said that "a functioning application should never, ever be written from the ground up." There's a cost in both time and effort to develop a new product. You give your competitors a chance to catch up because you're not able to devote that same time and resource to improving your existing product. There's also the risk that in rewriting your code, you'll leave out something that your customers will really miss.

Caudill concedes that there are times when you will be forced to recode a product—especially if your original code is keeping you from moving forward. "The conventional wisdom around rewriting software is that you should generally avoid it and make incremental improvements instead—unless that's truly impossible for some reason."

But, if you are forced to rewrite, what are your options?

Caudill points to Basecamp (https://basecamp.com/), the Chicago-based project management software company, as one example. The company had lots of ideas for how to improve their already wildly popular product, but users weren't interested in having their work disrupted by a change in the software. At the same time, data showed that they weren't signing up as many new users as they could because of the features they hadn't added yet. Rather than rewrite their entire solution, they decided to build a separate standalone product—Basecamp 2. They made no guarantee that the new product would have the same features as the old.

---

[1] Herb Caudill, "Lessons from 6 Software Rewrite Stories," Medium, February 19, 2019; https://medium.com/@herbcaudill/lessons-from-6-software-rewrite-stories-635e4c8f7c22

So how did they sell that to their existing customer base? They didn't. While they offered to transition any customers interested in moving to the new software, they also kept their old product alive—along with a guarantee that they would continue to support it indefinitely. Interestingly, the team did the same thing just a few years later with Basecamp 3. While it came with the cost of maintaining multiple versions of the software, the upside for the team was that they got to build the product they wanted. Plus, as Caudill writes, "For users, this is the best of both worlds: People who don't like change don't get their cheese moved, but people who are bumping against your product's limitations get to work with a new and, hopefully better thought-out application." While not every company has the resources to aggressively build new products like this, there is upside when you can.

A second example is FreshBooks (https://www.freshbooks.com/), which offers online invoicing software for small businesses. Though started by a nontechnical entrepreneur named Mike McDerment, the software was a hit. Within a decade, it had more than 10 million users. But engineers also struggled with what we call "founder's code," or legacy code that McDerment had paid people to create for him early on. Starting over, especially when people's finances are involved, can be very tricky business. So McDerment started a completely separate company called BillSpring—and he kept the fact that it was linked to FreshBooks a secret. He then gave his engineering team 4.5 months to develop a minimum viable product to test the market for the new software. Within a year, they had validation when a FreshBooks customer cancelled their account and signed up with BillSpring. After that, they let everyone know that BillSpring was an upgraded product and gave customers the option to migrate over.

As Caudill explains it: "FreshBooks went to extraordinary lengths to insulate themselves from the potential downside of a rewrite: By innovating under a throw-away brand, developers felt free to rethink things completely and to take bigger risks. That way, the worst that could happen was that they'd reach another dead end; at least they wouldn't damage their existing brand in the process."

But creating parallel products doesn't always work. One case in point is Inbox for Google. Google introduced this alternative user-interface for Gmail including new features that Gmail lacked. But users could still switch back and forth between the two products if they wanted. Eventually, though, Google killed Inbox but incorporated its most popular features, like inline attachments, into Gmail.

What Caudill likes about this approach is the focus on experimentation without disruption. "Inbox gave the Gmail team a way to experiment with features without disrupting workflows for the vast majority of users who didn't choose to switch over," he wrote. And yet, Google got a lot of pushback and criticism for killing the software, especially from people who liked it better than Gmail.

Still, it serves as an example of how product teams can navigate the tricky waters of retiring old features while introducing new ones, without completely disrupting current users. Caudill writes as a takeaway: "Once you've learned enough that there's a certain distance between the current version of your product and the best version of that product you can imagine, then the right approach is not to replace your software with a new version, but to build something new next to it—without throwing away what you have."

In other words, you don't always have to throw away the value that you created in your original product in order to innovate for the future.

That's why there is a fallacy that you can build something new for everyone. Your real goal should be first to build new features for a small subset of users who will be easy to convert. Then, you can move onto the next thing and the next, which eventually leads to a wave of new customers. It might take years to get there, but that's OK.

## SUMMARY

While at first it might seem counterintuitive to talk about retiring products and features—most product managers are builders at heart—it's a critical strategy for driving a better customer experience. The old axiom that less is more is often true when it comes to products. Ignoring code and features comes with a price, both in terms of the complexity of managing the product, as well as the murky experience it creates for the customer. But when it comes time to remove features, don't guess or rely on your gut—use the data to see what your users are really doing. The same is true when it comes to truly understanding what your users want from your product, which is our next topic to tackle.

# CHAPTER 14

# What Users Want

**M**ost product leaders would say that talking to customers is one of their most important responsibilities. Customer feedback is vital to any successful software product, and product teams should always strive to understand and incorporate the voice of the customer in everything they build. The challenge, of course, is reaching the right customers.

It can be difficult to recruit customers to provide feedback, especially if you don't have an existing relationship. And so most PMs will rely on the customers they already know to ask for feedback rather than trying to connect with unfamiliar ones. The problem with that strategy is that the most vocal customers aren't always the most representative ones. In fact, the things that make them vocal, such as an unusual or advanced use case, can actually make them the wrong customers to rely on for feedback.

The highest quality feedback typically comes from specific sets of users. For example, input on how to improve a certain feature should come from its most active users, whereas feedback on the onboarding process should come from users who are new to the product. Targeted outreach based on identified user behavior is key for getting quality feedback.

As a product leader, how can you gather better and more representative customer feedback? First, get out of your comfort zone and find users who accurately represent the customer population. And second, segment and target those customers based on the area of the product you wish to improve.

As companies grow, product teams must effectively scale, manage, and organize customer feedback. Each design, feature, and product update should be evaluated based on adoption and customer feedback. Product plans, priorities, and goals should then be adjusted, the next round of updates scoped, and the cycle begins again. Effective feedback programs are critical because they directly increase customer engagement and satisfaction. Yet there's no single, perfect feedback method.

## RUNNING HIGH VALUE USER TESTS

The same considerations made when connecting with customers for feedback should apply to those you are using for testing as well. User testing is extremely valuable, and something that product teams should do as frequently as possible. It provides valuable feedback on the user experience and helps to assess the impact of UI changes.

It's vital to recruit quality candidates for usability testing. Remember that every application has a "silent majority" of users. Look for great subjects that aren't necessarily already in your purview to get a full picture. You can also rely on product data to identify quality participants: for example, targeting users based on the time they've spent in the product, the length of time they've been a customer, or whether they use features related to the ones you're testing. Their functional or user roles or plan level can also be important. Take some time to assemble a profile of the ideal test subject before beginning your outreach.

## RECRUITING TESTERS FOR YOUR PRODUCT

There are two ways to go about recruiting testers for your product. Traditional outreach includes the use of phone and email, but these methods tend to have lower response rates. Customer advisory panels and focus groups often have better results. But note that you may hear from the loudest person in the room and miss valuable feedback from the less vocal participants.

In-app outreach can be a more effective route. It lets you recruit users as a seamless part of the product experience. Just be sure to target users based on product usage data rather than spamming your entire customer base.

Before you begin user testing, think about which tasks you'll include and the key metrics that you will need to collect. Will you be replacing an existing workflow? Is your focus on high-frequency or low-frequency tasks? What are your key outcomes and goals? What is your testing sequence? Defining these aspects will ensure that you are well prepared.

## GETTING BEYOND ONE-ON-ONE INTERVIEWS

When it comes to product feedback, nothing has more credibility with product managers than 1:1 interviews with customers or prospects. This is true whether you're trying to get insights that inform new capabilities or insights that refine existing ones.

Product managers in very early stage companies are especially familiar with the technique, as 1:1 interviews are generally the only source of customer insights they have. Most products are born out of a handful of early discussions with the right people. But for the SaaS or enterprise product manager, particularly those in companies that are actively scaling, relying on 1:1 interviews for their entire feedback diet just isn't realistic. This goes beyond some of the more obvious issues—they're time-consuming to set up and administer, data get stale, it's hard to share what has been learned across the product team—and gets to the heart of what it means to be a modern product manager.

Agile development moves fast, and product priorities can shift rapidly, so there is always a greater need for feedback than any team has bandwidth to solicit. Product managers, especially those who oversee freemium, consumer applications, or self-service products, have never been more outnumbered by customers. They're also constantly trying to serve different constituencies in ever more heterogeneous customer bases.

## GAPS WITH EXISTING FEEDBACK METHODS

Modern product managers want to find other sources of feedback beyond 1:1 interviews. Here are some of the new feedback strategies they are using to gain a solid understanding of customer needs:

1. In-app feedback surveys or polls can ask customers specific, focused questions and garner higher response rates than email since customers are being solicited while they're engaged with the product.
2. Survey tools can capture more in-depth information from customers and, if the questions are written well, they can enable a product manager to cut the resulting data in ways that don't just prove or disprove their hypothesis but also discover new insights.
3. NPS provides a shortcut to understanding how much customers like the product. Score fluctuations suggest when it's time to take a closer look at core functionality.
4. Customer Advisory Boards help to nurture long-term relationships with champions of your product. Members work in partnership with your product team to design the future of your product. They are also great for creating customer advocates.
5. Spreadsheets and other ad-hoc tools allow internal teams, like sales or customer success, to share product feedback they hear regularly from customers.

Combined, these activities help inform a deeper understanding of customer sentiment and needs. For example, a product manager can use the insights from in-app feedback to craft a survey that asks the most pressing questions about the product and then direct that survey to NPS detractors. Finding trends in this feedback could lead to ideas to help convert some detractors to promoters (or minimally, to neutrals), which increases sentiment overall.

Committing to take feedback seriously as a means to improve the product is a distinct advantage for product managers. However, there are a few issues to acknowledge:

- Internal teams have good instincts, but it's hard for the product team to make sense of "lots of people want—" without knowing who asked for it and exactly what they said.
- Users may not give enough feedback because they're unaware of how much it's wanted or how it affects product decisions.
- Teams can make it too hard ("Do you have time for a 10-minute survey?") and/or users can't see an obvious value ("What do I get out of filling this out?").

It's also helpful to note how easy it is for a user to ask for a feature. However, asking for the feature presupposes the solution. The more valuable feedback is the problem or "why" they want to solve. It's possible that the product team has considered alternate solutions to that problem that the customer hadn't considered. The solution may be a lot easier than just building what a user says they want.

Even if product managers do manage to overcome these feedback challenges, they often have a data aggregation problem. The product team struggles to maintain multiple spreadsheets of feedback or to organize thousands of pieces of raw feedback to reveal actionable insights.

## THE NEXT GENERATION OF FEEDBACK

To tackle these problems, some PMs create a single repository for all qualitative feedback, whether it's an NPS survey response, feedback about a beta feature, or a request to fill a perceived product gap. Ideally, this single repository:

- Is an always-on solution for customers or customer team members to enter feedback.
- Allows teams to map feedback to specific product areas, product gaps, or roadmap items.
- Makes it easy to close the loop with the person who gave the feedback and the internal team when there are follow-up questions or status changes.

There are a few different ways to create a single-source feedback database—in Salesforce, via Airtable, using Pendo, or with

UserVoice, for example. These tools can solve many of the issues mentioned earlier. They can help reduce and automate low-value work. One survey found that product managers without a feedback database spend about 20 to 25 percent of their time just organizing feedback from inside and outside the organization.

Having such a system gives a product manager a comprehensive database of feedback that is representative and credible. With a disorganized feedback mix, companies may only consume feedback from a small portion of their customers. With this approach, companies have the potential to map feedback from 50 percent of customers or more.

This feedback data is useful throughout the entire product development process:

- When looking at potential issues on a product roadmap, the team can easily see and understand which problems most affect specific customer segments.
- Ideas generated by management can be quickly validated (or invalidated) via existing feedback.
- Once mockups are created, teams have a readily available database of interested users to call on for testing.

Product teams are also able to conduct a meaningful analysis of the feedback in aggregate to answer questions like "What are we hearing most from Customer 1?" or "What is the potential revenue impact of choosing Feature A over Feature B?" These insights are connected to raw feedback and data from corresponding customers, enabling the product team to dig in and validate potential solutions quickly.

## MORE ENGAGED COMPANIES CREATE MORE ENGAGED CUSTOMERS

Finally (and maybe most importantly), product managers help develop more customer evangelists. In our experience, people are massively impressed when companies close the loop on product feedback, even if it's months later and the product team has decided not to act on it. Studies have found that only 5 percent of companies reliably respond to customer feedback. Don't discount how valuable it is to exceed these decidedly low expectations.

## MANAGING FEATURE REQUESTS

Anyone who's spent time working in product development can tell you: the requests never stop coming. There's always a steady stream of new ideas pouring in. And with so many unstructured requests arriving via so many different channels (for example, email, live chat, and support tickets), making calculated product decisions can, at first glance, seem impossible. As a result, some product leaders end up ignoring user feedback altogether. That just trades one problem for another.

While it's not necessarily crucial for product leaders to scrutinize every little suggestion that bubbles up, product-led companies match requests and invest time where there's density. We recommend assigning one (or more) owners to triage the incoming demand of requests. Generally, this triage should be fast, as the goal is to provide feedback to users quickly. Perhaps more important than building feedback is creating two-way communication with the customer—they just want to be heard. At one point, Atlassian (https://www.atlassian.com/) had a great program where their autoresponder to a feature request included a "thank you" and a brief summary of the upcoming roadmap. This improved user sentiment, and while it wasn't a commitment to build the request, the roadmap may have included ideas that the user wasn't considering but that would deliver significant value beyond the original request.

### How to Prioritize Top Feature Requests

As you sort and organize feature requests, you should consider both customer and market priorities. It helps to give users the option to weight the importance of their requests. Here are a few techniques that you can use:

**Basic votes**: Each user can vote for as many items as they desire.

**Weighted vote**: Each user gets a budget of votes, and they can allocate a relative value to different items.

**Pairwise voting**: Users are presented with two ideas and are asked which is more important.

Here are a few ways to measure their requests:

- Number of customers asking
- Number of users asking
- Sum of revenue for customers or users asking
- Sum of scores based on users

Of course, any of these measures can be segmented (see above) or trended (also see above) to understand patterns and deliver insights.

While different companies will take different approaches to prioritization, a uniting principle of product-led organizations is that feedback should be centralized. Your initial goal should be to create a centralized system where all of your feature requests are stored. This will make it considerably easier for you to understand the most common and pressing feature requests. At the end of the day, the goal of product management is to determine the top priorities, and it's best to evaluate this across the entire product. And, by analyzing feature requests at the user and account level with the help of tools like the one shown in Figure 14.1, you'll be able to identify patterns that can help you prioritize your work.

Regardless of how you manage your feature requests, always be sure to close the loop with the people who share feedback. It's not enough simply to analyze what users have told you; you have to let them know that their voices have been heard.

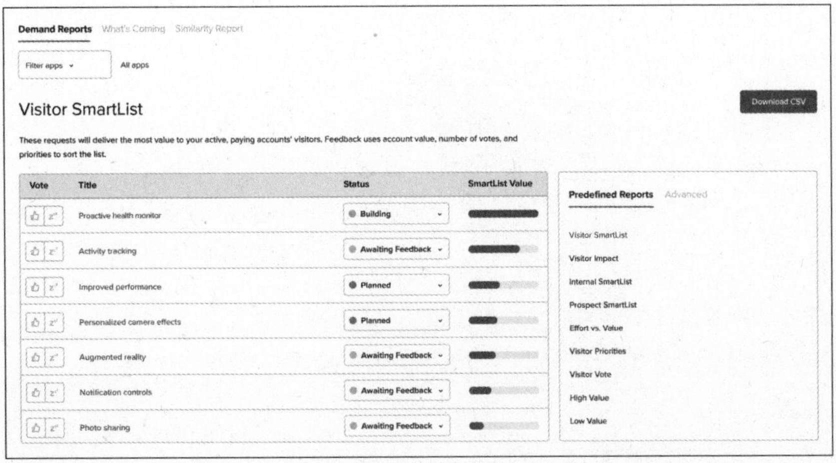

**FIGURE 14.1** Pendo's Feedback Tool
*Source:* Pendo

## MAINTAINING PRODUCT QUALITY AND EFFICIENCY

Some of the feedback you receive may address bugs in your product. For most digital product teams, bugs are inevitable, and they don't mean that your product is substandard. (And, conversely, having zero bugs doesn't necessarily mean users are going to love your product.) The most important thing isn't whether or not they arise, but how you deal with them. The best product leaders realize that they can't always *prevent* bugs, but they can ensure they're caught and fixed in a timely manner.

### How to Measure Product Bugs

There are two measurements that are most helpful for addressing bugs quickly and effectively. The first is to look at a breakdown of product bugs by feature (see Figure 14.2). This view helps you pinpoint the buggiest parts of your product and devote more resources to fixing the problems. As you prioritize which bugs you're going

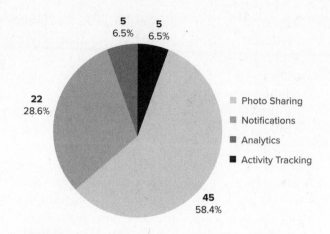

**FIGURE 14.2**   Product Bugs by Feature Chart
*Source:* Pendo

to fix first, it's also important to consider product usage. In order to deliver the best product experience to the greatest number of users, you should prioritize bugs found in the most heavily used areas of your product over those found in less popular areas.

The second measurement is the number of bugs reported versus the number of bugs you've fixed (see Figure 14.3). This is something you can chart over time. In a perfect world, you'd resolve bugs as

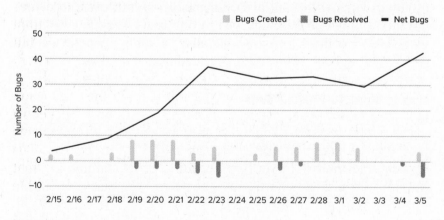

**FIGURE 14.3**   Bug Growth over Time Chart
*Source:* Pendo

quickly as they arise so that your net bug count remains at zero. Unfortunately, that's not the world we live in, which is why you need to track bugs reported versus bugs fixed—or net bugs. As a product leader, this allows you to evaluate how well you're maintaining the quality and efficiency of your product.

Bugs are a proxy for the overall quality of the product. If the quality of the product is noticeably poor, it will affect the user experience and overall success of the product. And it won't matter if what you're building is new and exciting—the lack of quality will overshadow the innovation. In some cases, you may consider "shutting down the line"—a phrase borrowed from Toyota's approach to lean manufacturing and continuous improvement—which means pausing or even stopping new feature development altogether to focus on fixing bugs.[1] Just as in a Toyota factory, where any worker on the line can stop production if they see an error, you want to ensure that your product delivers what your customers expect.

## MEASURING PRODUCT PERFORMANCE

In today's on-demand, one-click world—where you can buy just about anything online and have it delivered to your door in hours—people have come to expect products just to work and work fast. This expectation is especially acute in SaaS, where products perceived to be slow fall out of favor quickly. Even if users find your product valuable, they're always just one renewal cycle away from going with a competitor who can deliver a similar experience, but faster. Throughout my career, the feedback "it's slow" is a very common refrain (and I don't think it's specific to me personally).

To make product performance a top priority for your team, you need to set a goal for how quickly your product can return performance requests. You may want to identify an acceptable performance standard (say, requests delivered in five seconds or less) and then hold yourself accountable to maintaining that standard for a sizable portion of your customer base or a sizable

---

[1]Tommy Norman, "Stop the Line: How Lean Principles Safeguard Quality," LeanKit.com, October 26, 2016

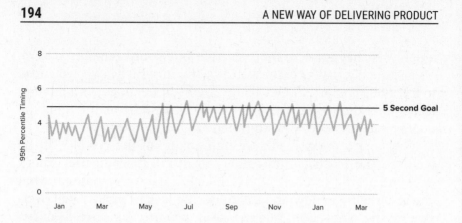

**FIGURE 14.4**   Product Performance over Time
*Source:* Pendo

percentage of all requests. However, keep in mind that some customers are larger than others and some use cases are more sophisticated. It's important to set performance standards specific to a use case and customer demographic. Once you establish an internal performance benchmark, measure yourself against it regularly. For example, Figure 14.4 depicts hypothetical product performance over time charted against a 5-second goal.

## SUMMARY

One of the eternal challenges faced by any product manager is finding effective ways to connect with users and turn their feedback into action that drives value. That gets even more difficult when you try to do it at scale. The good news is that there is a variety of different approaches, from running tests and collecting feedback from volunteers and customer advisory boards to developing automated approaches to managing customer feature requests, all with a goal of putting the customer experience at the center of your product. Another factor in fulfilling this objective, and the topic of the next chapter, is to embrace the practice of dynamic roadmapping, where you help your users and your product-led organization see where you're heading into the future.

# CHAPTER 15

# Dynamic Roadmapping

Every new project or product starts with a plan. In this case, we're talking about a roadmap, which is something I have relied on throughout my career. As product teams decide what to build next, business strategy, market data, usage data, and customer interviews inform any product enhancements. Features are scoped, priorities are set, and success metrics are defined.

One of the primary jobs of a product manager is to refine a massive universe of possible investment candidates into the few that will have the greatest impact for customers and the business. If there are a hundred features an organization could build, most companies are resourced to invest in only a handful. That can feel like an exercise with nearly impossible tradeoffs, where the difference between one bet and another can have enormous but unknowable implications for the customer and company. It can feel like a high-stakes gamble.

This is why the *product roadmap* isn't just a document; it's a powerful planning, communication, and organizational alignment tool. It reflects the product team's plan for what is going to happen in the future, based on current priorities. It's a summarized, often thematic view of the force-ranked backlog, and it provides a useful way for product teams to share current plans. It is, as the safe harbor statement points out, nonbinding and always "subject to change."

There are many different styles of roadmaps product managers should consider. The most common style takes the form of a Gantt chart, which depicts blocks of time stacked from left to right, as you can see in a sample chart in Figure 15.1. Each block is a task, and stacking them allows you to visualize which tasks are dependent on each other or how many different tasks you might be running in parallel.

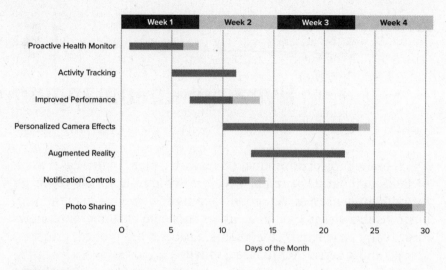

**FIGURE 15.1**   Sample Gantt Chart
*Source:* Pendo

The scope of time shown in the chart depends on the organization—it can stretch over months, quarters, or even years.

What is so effective about a visualization like this is that it communicates what the product team thinks is the most important thing to work on at the given time. The chart can also help highlight when a team may have overcommitted by working on 10 things at once—which rarely works well—as opposed to a narrower list of tasks. Visualizing the work helps the team to really home in on the most important thing to work on.

That's also why I like to create a force-ranked list of tasks to help everyone stay focused on the most important task, followed by the second, the third, and beyond.

The number one reason I like creating roadmaps is that they are an effective way to communicate with internal and external stakeholders about the purpose of your product and then to solicit their feedback. Not only do you want to collect that from customers, but also from your sales and customer-facing teams, as a way to get them to buy into the vision for the product. It gives them a sense of the direction of where the company is headed.

When it comes to communicating with your customers, roadmaps can be an effective way to start a productive conversation. You get two very different reactions if you ask a customer what they want from the product versus asking for feedback on what you tell them that you want to build.

Roadmaps also help you communicate with customers about priorities. If they want the development of a particular feature prioritized, they will likely have to bump something else down in priority. It forces them to think about tradeoffs, especially when you use a force-ranked list. One of the pro tips I've learned is to be honest about telling customers that the longer things are pushed out into the future, the less likely they are ever going to get built. New priorities always arrive as the market changes.

The real question is, How should the product team arrive at the key priorities in the first place? Product managers have no shortage of input, especially if you work in a product-led organization. Vocal customers, executives, and sellers all have opinions on what should be built next. The challenge is sorting through all of that feedback to prioritize what truly delivers customer value. This requires data.

Data-driven product managers incorporate KPIs and strategic goals into their roadmaps and backlog prioritization. They use data to identify opportunities for product enhancement, to inform prioritization decisions, and to measure the uptake and impact of new features and new products.

First, however, you need to identify the right metrics to guide the roadmap.

## START WITH VISION AND STRATEGY

Before prioritizing any feature in the backlog, it's important to be sure that it is aligned with the overall business strategy and vision. It's hard to effectively prioritize what to build if the broad objectives are unclear. What's the market pain that you're trying to address? Who is the target customer, their industry, and their persona? What is the market opportunity? Where do you see the best opportunity for growth? These are key strategic questions that must be addressed before any feature-level discussions can happen.

When developing a strategy that ultimately leads to a product roadmap, it's important to identify and articulate the product's vision and principles—the why. Product teams need to spend time before they begin planning the roadmap to determine the product's mission and then distill it into a simple statement that stakeholders can understand. This includes product vision, the problems that it solves, its target customers, and its value to the marketplace. Documenting this process forces the product manager to nail down many of the key items that will inform the roadmap.

The executive team needs to know (and agree with) the plan for the product's development and updates because they will ultimately need to sign off on those plans. Development teams need to know what the product team has planned for the product, and why, because they will be responsible for building it. The sales, service, and marketing teams will need to know the vision as well so that they can articulate the go-to-market strategy for the product. This strategy-first approach has several benefits:

- By articulating the product vision across the company, the product team can ensure that the stakeholders are on the same page before product managers begin the detailed conversations to follow.
- A clear product vision allows the entire product team to identify priorities for their products, as well as set aside items or ideas that don't serve the vision.

From the product vision, product managers can derive product goals that will in turn influence the initiatives that are on the roadmap. Coming up with product goals is the step that helps the product manager translate product strategy into an executable plan. Every organization's product goals will be different. Teams can develop product-specific, company-oriented, or more generic goals. Here are some examples:

- Competitive Differentiation
- Customer Delight

- Technical Improvements
- Sustain Product Features
- Improve Customer Satisfaction
- Increase Lifetime Value
- Upsell New Services
- Reduce Churn
- Expand Geographically
- Mobile Adoption

These goals are general, but they can usually be measured and tied back to metrics and Key Performance Indicators (KPIs). It's these types of goals that will resonate with the product's stakeholders. Goals are often longer-term initiatives. For example, they might change annually rather than monthly. These metrics serve as the baseline for any product initiative and should be reflected in roadmap priorities.

## PRIORITIZE APPROPRIATELY

Effective prioritization is a continuing challenge for product teams. Engineering resources are always limited, forcing product teams to focus on maximizing customer value with every feature delivered. The question we've addressed over the course of this chapter is how to know which item on the roadmap will deliver the most value.

Data-driven, product-led teams should consider both the alignment with strategic objectives as well as customer behavior and input to arrive at prioritization decisions. For example, the online educational company Coursera (https://www.coursera.org/) analyzed user behavior to help prioritize what features to build in time for their annual user conference. The team that works on the educator side of the platform decided to make incremental updates to their most trafficked page, where courses are created. They weren't massive changes, but they made a big impact for their users, who found it easier and faster to navigate the page.

At a basic level, understanding how much an existing feature or area of the product is used should inform whether to invest additional development resources. Prioritizing feature updates for things that are rarely used is not likely to deliver significant value. However, a feature may be underused because it doesn't provide value or because it's difficult to use. Adding targeted customer feedback into the analysis can help determine the why behind observed behavior and further refine feature prioritization.

For net new products or features, it may be difficult to rely on historical customer behavior alone to drive prioritization. For these decisions, product teams should rely more heavily on alignment with vision and strategy. The key questions here are: Does this feature further our strategic objectives moreso than the next best option, and how would we measure that? Though any prioritization decision is, at some level, a "best guess" measurement, data can inform the decision. It should also be leveraged to evaluate the decision once the feature or product is built.

## ASSIGN SPECIFIC METRICS TO EACH ITEM IN YOUR ROADMAP

A product investment has no place in the product roadmap if you can't assess its value. Product teams should be sure to assign both business (for instance, revenue) and adoption/usage goals to each prioritized feature.

Business metrics like revenue, churn, or conversion rate represent higher-level outcomes mapped to goals that a product team is hoping to achieve. Customer-oriented or usage metrics are specific measures of behavior or user sentiment that can be leading indicators of business outcomes. Roadmap initiatives should be associated with specific goals for both business and usage.

### Measure Your Impact

To understand impact, each roadmap feature should have baseline KPIs associated with it. Those could be usage (this feature should be used by X% of users in 30 days), usability and customer satisfaction (these UI changes should reduce support requests by X%), or specific financial metrics (migrate 20 additional accounts to a paid tier). The KPIs should be set ahead of time and integrated within the roadmap itself. That way, you can ensure that any development required to support measurement is scoped as part of the feature and that the organization understands how the product team is measuring success.

## Communicating Priorities

In most Agile product development organizations, the backlog defines the product features for the near term. From the backlog, the development team is (hopefully) aware of what's coming next, at least for the next few sprints or iterations.

But the backlog in itself is not the roadmap—a product roadmap gives a strategic view of where the product is headed over the mid to long term. The roadmap is tied to the organization's vision and strategic goals, often for the next 12 or more months. In an Agile organization, the roadmap provides guidance rather than a strict project plan.

The roadmap needs to communicate the big picture to the organization—the initiatives that expand markets, address competition, and create customer value. That big-picture thinking can't be distilled in the backlog—it's challenging to communicate strategy in a list that's 200 items long, especially to executives and other stakeholders who might not think in terms of iterations or sprints.

The goal of a roadmap is to provide an organized view of development priorities. It is only effective as a communication tool if it can convey the why behind the priorities it illustrates. Effective product teams know that incorporating goals and metrics into the roadmap documents helps to illustrate the why. It also makes the team accountable for results. Too often roadmaps are shared without any of this explanation or reasoning. If details cannot be included, product leaders should simply avoid sharing a roadmap until they've talked through the items and priorities with the rest of the organization or stakeholders.

One danger area for roadmaps is presenting something that commits engineers to a particular oath if they haven't been involved in the planning process. I've been involved in presentations where a product manager is showing a PowerPoint of the roadmap while engineers in the audience are scowling because they didn't commit to anything they're seeing. Roadmaps are only effective if they align and focus everyone involved in achieving the work.

## How to Measure Product Delivery Predictability

In addition to being able to predict how users will behave, strong product leaders can also anticipate how their team will perform. Without that predictability, product leaders run the risk of publishing a roadmap the team can't rely on.

Of course, part of the reason for publishing your roadmap is to create a sense of accountability within your team and alignment with adjacent functions, particularly R&D. That's why it's essential that your roadmap blends art (what your experience tells you is possible) with science (what the data indicates is probable) to paint a realistic picture of the future.

Here's a scenario I've heard from product leaders: The executive team reviews a product roadmap dashboard every two weeks (assuming two-week sprint cycles). The product team measures predictability by taking the ratio of the number of story points completed to the number of story points the product team originally committed to. The resulting percentages reveal, roadmap item by roadmap item, whether the team is behind, on schedule, or ahead of schedule. As a product leader, you can use these types of findings to build a more informed roadmap—one you can have greater confidence in (see Figure 15.2).

| P | Team | Roadmap Item | Fcst | S45 | S46 | S47 | S48 |
|---|------|--------------|------|-----|-----|-----|-----|
| 1 | A | Proactive Health Monitor | | 71% | 222% | 514% | 225% |
| 2 | B | Comprehensive Activity Tracking | | 56% | 110% | 100% | 1335% |
| 3 | B | Improved Performance | | | | | |
| 5 | C | Personalized Camera Effects | | 36% | 100% | 100% | 109% |
| 6 | D | Augmented Reality | | 58% | 91% | 132% | 127% |
| 7 | E | Notification Controls | | 122% | 182% | 108% | 121% |
| 8 | E | Photo Sharing | | | | | |

**FIGURE 15.2** Product Roadmap Snapshot
*Source:* Pendo

## ROADMAPS ARE NEVER STATIC

A roadmap is never "done." Elements are always changing. A roadmap should be agile and treated as a living document—not a fixed plan. Product teams should expect to regularly revisit, discuss, and reprioritize the roadmap based on new inputs. And so, any roadmap discussion is an opportunity to gain feedback. That feedback isn't always actionable, and it may not cause a change in priorities, but it's an important way to see how the thing you're building is perceived by the market and your customers.

Because the roadmap will inevitably change, it's important to set the expectation with stakeholders that the roadmap is not a promise.

Many of our customers keep their roadmap dates at a monthly or quarterly level or leave the dates off altogether to avoid setting the expectation that features will be delivered by a specific date.

Product managers need to communicate regularly where the product is heading so that everyone is on the same page, especially the stakeholders who make final decisions, control the budget, or influence the direction of the company. An Agile product roadmap, therefore, should be a visual, easy-to-digest document that stakeholders can understand and that gives perspective to the backlog.

## PRACTICAL ROADMAP TAKEAWAYS

One aspect of roadmaps that doesn't get talked about often is the assumption that when a product is shipped, teams can remove it from the roadmap. In other words, once the task of shipping the product on your Gantt chart is done, it frees you up to move on to something else. But what if the product you shipped doesn't meet customer expectations? Or what if it fails to address the strategic business case you established in the beginning? In either case, you are certainly not done with that product. You need to keep working on it until it does, in fact, match your customers' or business's expectations. That's why you need to build tasks and time commitments into your roadmap to measure outcomes. You need to determine whether you achieved the expected result and whether the product provided the benefits customers hoped for.

That also speaks to the importance of keeping your roadmaps up to date. Things will always change. Having a current and updated roadmap is critical for keeping up with those changes.

One thing I've learned over the course of my career is that you can't get emotionally tied to your roadmap. Too often, I've seen product teams invest time and energy creating a roadmap they believe in, but all they're looking for is a stamp of approval. When a customer gives pushback, they resist making changes to the roadmap. They're unwilling to change it because they think it's "perfect." In other words, they've now adopted a "fixed" mindset that blinds them to new opportunities.

For example, if a customer makes a request and says that they are willing to pay you a lot of money to prioritize it, should you stick to the roadmap and say no, or should you consider that good feedback to work with? This is a case where someone is willing to vote with their dollars on a feature they want, which can be worth far more than someone just sharing an opinion with you. You can see how changing your roadmap may sometimes be a good thing, something you want to embrace.

Another question about roadmaps that I've heard over the years is whether to publish the roadmap publicly, say, on a web page or a wiki. I've done this before—after we got our engineers to commit to the plan, we published our roadmap for anyone to see. But after we released a major architectural change, the release didn't work. It was a failure. But we found ourselves stuck because we had set expectations based on a roadmap we couldn't deliver on. That's a dangerous place to be. Granted, development isn't a perfect science. Technology changes and humans make mistakes. It's impossible to consider every single use case out there. That's why you should use caution if you are going to publish your roadmap publicly.

In some scenarios, however, you might not have a choice. The open-source world tends to publish its roadmaps publicly. That community appreciates and even expects that level of transparency. If you are operating in that world, or even competing against it, you may be forced to share your roadmap. But if you do share it with the world, be sure you have confidence that you can execute against the plan. For example, some companies know that they are behind in the market and want to prove that they have a plan to catch up, so they may publish their roadmap. Meanwhile, other organizations might not be quite clear about their priorities beyond the next three months—they may want to keep their roadmap private.

What you share about your roadmap also depends on the audience. Boards of directors of companies like to see roadmaps to understand where the company is headed. But they don't need to see the same level of feature granularity and detail a customer might be interested in. A board will be more interested in the macro changes planned for the future. As with any communication tool, you need to know your audience and build the roadmap in a way that will best connect with them.

One of the root challenges with communicating a roadmap is granularity. Different audiences desire different levels of detail. Many customers, or users, simply want to know "Are you building my request?" which could be a tiny feature. Boards of directors, on the other hand, typically care about large initiatives since those reflect strategy and investments. I've found that it's best to have multiple versions of roadmaps for different audiences rather than attempt to create a single version for all.

Generally speaking, when it comes to sharing your roadmap, I am not a fan of sending it via email. As I said before, the key role of the roadmap is to communicate and to collect feedback through conversations—that's where the real magic happens. That can be difficult to accomplish in an email. That's why I like to share roadmaps in a presentation, where you can create a forum and hear complaints and critiques in real time. That dynamic drives better communication—and better products.

## SUMMARY

One of the most important jobs of a product manager is mapping the future of your product. The embodiment of that work is your organization's product roadmap, which helps point the direction you, and your customers, want to go in the future. It's the big picture everyone is driving toward. But creating a dynamic roadmap informed by data isn't just about aligning your external stakeholders—it should also rally teams inside your organization around a shared vision. As such, it is crucial for product managers to get buy-in throughout the organization. It's also important to remember that roadmapping is never complete; it never ends. That brings us to the topic of our final chapter, the rise of product operations (product ops) and the new makeup of product teams inside product-led companies. These teams help ensure that our companies deliver the best possible experience for our customers.

# CHAPTER 16

# Building Modern Product Teams

**M**ost product managers are aware of the mantra that we "lead through influence and not authority." Yet many entered their roles with very little guidance on what this means and how to apply it within their organizations. From the work we have done surveying hundreds of product leaders, a clear theme has emerged: product teams that can create strong alignment with the various stakeholders within their organizations build the most successful products and companies.

Back in Section Two, we discussed how to put product at the center of the customer experience. For that to happen, product teams must have influence and alignment with the entire organization. Modern product teams need to see themselves as orchestrators of the product-led company, helping each department leverage the product to deliver a better customer experience.

## PRODUCT MANAGERS LEAD THROUGH INFLUENCE

It is extremely rare for a product manager to be in a position with direct reports. Product managers don't hold the purse strings to decide who gets a bonus, raise, or promotion. Product managers don't perform annual reviews of the people they rely on to get their jobs done. Rather, product managers have to demonstrate leadership in the purest sense—we must inspire people to follow our lead; we must lead people to make the decisions we think are best; we must align different perspectives, so they're all fixed on the same goal.

Leading through influence is the defining characteristic of a truly great product manager—getting others to support your initiatives without becoming a bulldog or, worse, a bull in a china shop. Unfortunately, it isn't a skill that's taught in most undergraduate or graduate programs, or even in classroom-based product management certifications. It's a skill that develops over time, and all too often through trial and error by a newly minted product manager tossed into the deep end with little or no guidance. There are positives and negatives to this way of learning. Once the skill is mastered, a product manager isn't really a manager but a true leader. The downside is how difficult it is to know if you're doing it right due to the weeks or months it can take to see an impact. If our efforts misdirect or hamper the team, we might not be able to correct them immediately because we don't always know that the train is on the wrong track until it arrives at the wrong station.

Leading through influence rather than authority makes product management a job that is as much about understanding people as it is about understanding a market or a product. It becomes an exercise in establishing and maintaining relationships based on mutual trust and respect—relationships that must survive the most difficult times—so that we can right the ship after an emergency and continue sailing toward the North Star of our overarching vision. Product managers, perhaps more than any other role in the organization, succeed or fail not only on the merits of their own work, but on their ability to influence and motivate others.

When you look at the forces shaping the product manager role—heightened expectations on the customer experience, the growing availability of product usage data, and, most notably, the enormous advantage product-led companies have over their competition—it's clear that product managers need help to orient their entire organization around the product. That brings us to "Product Ops," a role with increasing importance in product-led organizations.

## THE RISE OF PRODUCT OPS

The concept of product operations or Product Ops isn't necessarily new, but it isn't exactly commonplace either. And, in fact, having a person in this role is less important than ensuring that the work is happening on product teams. Right now, it's one-tenth of one person's job and maybe one-fifth of another person's job. Product Ops is focused on identifying a specific role and people who own these important facets of what it takes to run a successful product team. For technology companies that are scaling, it can be the difference between successful growth and growing pains. It's simultaneously novel (applying the ruthless efficiency of sales operations to the R&D function) and familiar (what successful company doesn't have an ops function?).

You don't hear about Product Ops as often as you hear about marketing operations (Marketing Ops), sales operations (Sales Ops), or their amalgam, revenue operations (RevOps). Even development operations (DevOps) is prevalent throughout tech. But we think this could change, and Product Ops could soon find itself on equal footing with its popular predecessors.

Product Ops exists at the intersection of product, engineering, and customer success. It aspires to support the R&D team and

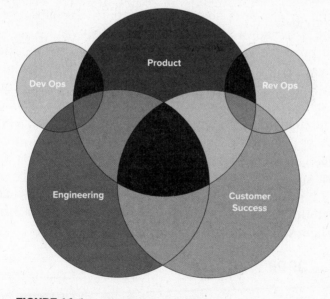

**FIGURE 16.1**  Operations Graphic
*Source*: Pendo

their go-to-market counterparts to tighten product feedback loops, systematize product development and launches, and scale product knowledge across the company. If it's a defined role, Product Ops typically sits in the product management team or an adjacent function that also reports up to the head of product.

Some companies may view Product Ops as a role to hire. Others may view it as a skillset that any product professional can (and should) hone. I see it as both: product-led organizations should designate someone to be responsible for Product Ops, but, at the same time, all members of the product team should develop an operational mindset.

Our annual survey of product managers shows that more than half of product teams now have a dedicated product operations function to wrangle data in support of better product decisions, to coordinate internal and external launches and communications, and to orchestrate the right messages and experiences inside the product. In addition to the 52 percent who have already built this function, another 19 percent have plans in the works to build up this capability. Fewer than 30 percent of teams expect product operations to remain a shared responsibility. Perhaps, unsurprisingly, the data shows a strong correlation between company size and the presence of a stand-alone Product Ops function, with 96 percent of companies over $1 billion in revenue reporting the presence of a dedicated Product Ops resource compared with just 17 percent under $25 million in revenue. Studies have found product-led companies' profit margin exceeds peers by upwards of 527 percent, and product-led companies are disproportionately likely to employ a Product Ops leader or even an entire team.

Let's have a look at each function the Product Ops team performs: Optimization, Alignment, Feedback Loops, and Infrastructure and Reporting.

## Optimization

Varun Ramamurthy Dinakur, the founder and CEO of hansel.io (https://hansel.io/) described product operations' value in audiophile terms. He said the volume knob is the product, whereas the equalizer settings are the Product Ops function. Product Ops informs the "tweaks and configurations" needed for the ideal product experience—in other words, optimizations.

In order to optimize the product experience, Product Ops is often responsible for collecting, structuring, and distributing customer feedback, whether it's been submitted directly through the product itself or indirectly via support tickets or in conversations with sales or account managers. Fragmented feedback increases the odds that even if the company is building quality products, they may not be building the right products.

In the product manager survey that Pendo conducts annually (which we have referenced throughout the book), a full 70 percent of product managers at companies with Product Ops resources indicated that they were able to successfully collect feedback and report it to stakeholders, whereas at companies without Product Ops, the success rate dipped to 45 percent. Product Ops ties the product team more closely to the customer, which is why "customer-centricity" is an essential trait to screen for when hiring for this specialized role.

Ops can also help product teams increase the "hit rate" for new product and feature releases. By owning product usage and feedback data, and then reconciling it with account data in sales and marketing databases, Product Ops enables the launch teams to make smarter decisions regarding rollout strategies. They can advise on which customer profiles lend themselves to beta testers, discern who is most likely to become an early adopter, and even figure out which customer cohorts have the potential to be public advocates for the new offer. Product Ops can tilt the odds in favor of the company.

The same holds true for the reciprocal issue: that is, sunsetting features. Product teams are often concerned with the unintended consequences associated with prematurely retiring a feature or retiring the wrong feature. Making a mistake could have devastating consequences on product usage, user satisfaction, and even customer renewal. As a result, features that should be retired linger, contributing to feature bloat and ultimately compromising the entire product experience.

A data-focused Product Ops leader can help product managers understand which features deliver value, which cause friction, which correlate to satisfaction, and which drive down customer happiness. Just as Product Ops can help product managers make the right decisions when launching new features, they can also help their colleagues avoid the wrong decisions when sunsetting.

The ultimate outcome is better products that deliver more value to users while removing friction from the product experience.

## Alignment

*"The connective tissue between teams."*

That's how Blake Samic, Head of Product Operations at Stripe, describes the impact that product operations has on cross-functional alignment.

Just as revenue operations sits at the center of the broader go-to-market team, product operations is the nexus of product, engineering, and customer success as well as adjacent operations functions like development ops and revenue ops.

Because it's positioned at the hub of so many business functions, Product Ops can add considerable value to cross-departmental alignment and communications. It can liaise with its operational counterparts to enrich product usage, feedback, and NPS data with sales, marketing, and finance data to produce timely or hidden insights for executive leadership. Product Ops managers can help ensure that engineering understands the *why* behind what they're building; meanwhile, it can shepherd stories from the customer success team to the product team to enrich data with real-life customer narratives.

Aligning with each line of business puts Product Ops in a position to scope business needs at the beginning of the product development process, which, yet again, helps tilt the odds in favor of success when planning a future release.

In most cases, data is the Product Ops payload when the team is communicating cross-departmentally. Product Ops brings data to help colleagues improve their performance—for example, helping the marketing team understand which customer cohorts are most likely to be receptive to a forthcoming product—and shares data and anecdotes with the product team to enrich their understanding of the buyer. Companies that have invested in Product Ops resources are enjoying virtuous cycle benefits. They are achieving significantly clearer communication and collaboration between R&D and the go-to-market function (70 percent are satisfied) as opposed to those without the function (37 percent are satisfied).

How might Product Ops align with others across the company? Here are a few possibilities:

- Aligning with RevOps to ensure that product data is incorporated into business health metrics, such as trial conversions and customer renewals and expansions.
- Teaming with customer success to paint a more complete customer picture by reconciling usage data, feature requests, and sentiment scores with support tickets and front-line call experiences.
- Taking this "complete customer picture" to sales and marketing to hone persona definitions so that the company can pursue the types of customers who are most likely to enjoy success.
- Defining performance experience metrics in partnership with the QA team to measure success around the product experience better.

## Feedback Loops

As discussed in the alignment section above, Product Ops is responsible for exchanging data and intel with adjacent departments. But it's also responsible for feedback loops between the product team and the customer.

In one sense, the presence of Product Ops alone liberates the product managers to spend more time in the field. So, Product Ops starts off with assist points. But by refining data into insights and feeding that intelligence back into the product function, the Product Ops specialist helps give rise to smarter, faster decision making.

Melissa Perri, founder of Produx Labs and a prominent voice in modern product management, said, "Product Ops needs to be able to get leadership the data that they need to make product decisions, not just the data they ask for."

Tight feedback loops can begin to resemble "product enablement," the data, stories, and guidance required to ensure that product managers are not only building the right solutions, but also prioritizing the most critical improvements of existing products. Sometimes, customers don't want the new thing; they just want the thing they have to work better. It's in this capacity that Product Ops plays a key role in escalation. By correlating usage with satisfaction, such as NPS, they can help product managers know when a fix supersedes a build.

Whether the priority is placed on developing something new or improving something that already exists, reliable decisions follow smart experiments—and Product Ops is charged with removing friction from the experimentation process, allowing product managers to run more experiments and thus help the business scale.

Product operations teams keep track of every active experiment and make sure that tests aren't overlapping or interfering with each other. They may also document repeatable processes to introduce greater efficiency and reliability into the experimentation process.

### Infrastructure and Reporting

All this data requires infrastructure, and Product Ops is responsible for selecting, integrating, maintaining, and operating the product team's tech stack—product usage analytics, product guides, feedback collection, roadmapping, and integrations with other departments' systems of record. This all falls within the purview of product operations.

As the infrastructure owner, the product operations leader is also responsible for demonstrating the business value of each tool in the stack, ensuring that the company is deriving value from its technology investments. Combating tool sprawl is an easily overlooked priority.

Owning a tech stack typically goes hand in hand with owning reporting, and product operations is no exception. Product Ops is typically responsible for compiling the product team's quarterly business review and reporting for boards of directors, where they provide a quantifiable and measurable perspective on product health. These presentations map to the product team's strategy and vision and highlight many of the KPIs discussed throughout this book. Metrics like product stickiness, feature adoption, app retention, and NPS taken together provide leadership with a multidimensional view of product health.

## MOVING PRODUCT TO THE CENTER OF THE ORGANIZATION

Product teams have a very wide range of roles and responsibilities—they own functions from engineering to marketing and sales. Yet, traditionally, they haven't had a defined C-level leadership role, most likely reporting to other operational or marketing leadership functions. But as more of the customer journey (for business software in particular) takes place within the product and the product experience becomes a driver of business outcomes, companies are elevating product leadership to a more visible and responsible position within the senior leadership team. More often than ever, product has a seat at the table, and like their colleagues in sales, revenue, and marketing, they all need that ops function to ensure that the product team and the broader organization is aligned around the product.

## SUMMARY

Over the preceding chapters, we discussed how organizations need to evolve their relationship with users in order to deliver an optimal customer experience. And while we have discussed the many tools and techniques that you can employ to meet that goal, you must also evolve your own organization to put product at the center. The orchestrator of that is Product Ops. By rethinking the role your product plays inside your organization and considering how it ties every other functional area of the business together, you can begin to kickstart your own transformation into becoming a product-led organization.

# Conclusion: A Call to Action

This book is designed to take you on a journey—a journey to becoming a product-led organization. And that journey requires you to be willing to make changes and shift your thinking. What has worked in the past is not going to help your business grow and be successful in the future. If you want to build or remain a thriving company, you need to realize the power of your product to drive your customers' experience. As product teams continue to gain more influence, it will be up to product leaders like you to steer everyone within your organization toward this product-led approach.

The product-led movement is blurring the lines between product, engineering, marketing, sales, and customer success. The product team's responsibilities used to be limited to shipping features, but it now falls on their shoulders to partner with sales and marketing to reimagine the product as an acquisition tool, to collaborate with customer success to employ the product as a vehicle for onboarding and retention, and to ensure that executives view product analytics alongside revenue data as they make strategic decisions.

The role of product is changing. Product features are giving way to customer experiences, and in order to deliver meaningful ones, today's product leaders need to form a new set of skills and build new habits. Fortune favors the bold. The first to adapt to this shift will be rewarded.

Some have already begun to embrace this new world of product management. Consider that an executive of a major global car rental agency was promoted from CIO to Chief Product Development Officer, with a focus on creating digital products. Why? Because he and the company recognize that the only way to stay ahead of their competition is to put product at the center of everything they do—to become product led. Make no mistake: If you don't think your competitors are shifting to a product-led strategy, you may already be falling behind.

But it's not too late to get started. And you don't have to do everything I've suggested in the preceding pages all at once. Start incrementally. And start with data. Remember, you can't improve something if you aren't measuring it. So, establish some measures and benchmarks and tie them to your why, or where you want to go.

Once you've got a foundation built with data, shift to thinking about how your product sits at the center of your customers' experience. Are there ways to rethink how you deliver that experience, shifting from relying on human intervention to more of an automated approach inside your product? Remember that customers want a simple experience, and they want to be in control of it. Ask yourself how your product can begin to deliver more of what your customers want.

Finally, think about your own organization and how it's aligned with a product-led approach. Do you have the right team in place looking at the right measures to drive your growth? Do you have the customer at the center of your vision for where you want to go in the future? And are you co-creating that future alongside those customers, collecting and applying their feedback at every step of your product development?

One of Pendo's core values is "Bias to Act." When I explain this to new employees in each onboarding class, I share stories of colleagues asking for forgiveness rather than permission. I encourage individuals not to assume that someone else has created something that they believe is needed. This value has fueled many great programs and product capabilities at Pendo because it democratizes decision making to each individual.

That same principle applies to you. Now is the time for you to act. Do not assume that someone else is helping evolve your team and organization. I wrote this book as a way to inspire you to act before it's too late—before someone else forces you to change or before your competitors pass you by. This is your opportunity to change your mindset when it comes to product and to rethink how your product can transform your customers' entire experience with your company. When it comes to building products, companies will never be the same.

# Acknowledgments

When Wiley approached me to write a book, it felt like a really good idea. Having never written a book, I thought mostly of the end result—not the effort needed to create it. While I had a strong point of view and a set of ideas about what it means to be a product-driven company, putting those ideas onto paper and making it interesting and compelling was a more challenging proposition than I had anticipated. Thankfully, I had a strong team of support helping me craft this first book.

My marketing team at Pendo was my greatest support. They were consistently cajoling, reminding, writing, and helping me in this process. Thank you for your patience. I can admit that I tend to know what I want at times yet have challenges explaining it. Jake Sorofman was my first primary partner in this effort, and I'll forever remember those drafting sessions. Laura Baverman did so much behind-the-scenes effort to help make this a reality. Joe Chernov provided added support and content to help finalize the project.

The design team at Pendo—specifically Jess Vavra—did amazing work producing the graphics.

Darren Dahl came into the project after a few months, and I can confidently say changed the trajectory of it. Your patience and flexibility in working around my schedule and style helped take a nearly stream-of-consciousness set of stories and ideas and organize that into this cogent story. I also thank our editorial team at Wiley, especially Gary Schwartz, who served as my primary editor.

Aside from writing a book, I have a day job running a high-growth startup. My team stepped up to allow me to focus on finalizing this book. Jamie Brown, who runs my life, arranged my schedule so I could complete this project. Stephanie Brookby helped take key initiatives off my plate. Our leadership team, and frankly the more than 400 people at Pendo, helped make this book a reality.

Nearly seven years ago, Eric Boduch, Rahul Jain, and Erik Troan joined me to create a product to help measure and improve the effectiveness of software products. I had experienced this pain firsthand and had a sense of how we could solve this problem better than existing solutions. It's been an incredible ride so far, and it's amazing how we've maintained and grown our relationships throughout this process. I appreciate your efforts, encouragement, and tough words when I've needed them.

Many of the stories and ideas throughout this book come from organizations, teams, and people at product-led organizations. Your innovative spirit inspired and fueled my efforts in this book. Keep iterating and improving.

Far from last, I wanted to acknowledge my wife, Laura, and children, Mickey, Eva, Stella, Anders, and Annika, for all the sacrifice they made to help me complete this book. Writing this book was additive to my schedule, and they picked up extra chores to help free me up to complete this. It's much appreciated.

—Todd Olson

# About the Author

Todd Olson is co-founder and CEO of Pendo, a platform that accelerates and deepens software product adoption. A three-time entrepreneur, Todd has experienced the highs and lows of running fast-growth technology companies. His first venture-backed startup shut down during the dotcom era; his second was sold to Rally Software, where he stayed on as vice president of products through its IPO. His third is Pendo, which he founded with fellow product leaders and technologists from Red Hat, Cisco, and Google in October 2013. At publication, Todd and team have raised $206 million in venture capital, landed more than 1500 customers, and now employ 450 people across six offices around the globe. Todd lives in Raleigh, North Carolina with his wife and four children.

# Index